THE SADHAK

HYPNOTIC HINDI LANGUAGE LEARNINGS
TAUGHT IN A LOVE STORY

Bryan James Westra

Indirect Knowledge Limited
MURRAY, KENTUCKY

Copyright © 2014 Bryan James Westra.

All rights reserved. No part of this publication may be reproduced, distributed or transmitted in any form or by any means, including photocopying, recording, or other electronic or mechanical methods, without the prior written permission of the publisher, except in the case of brief quotations embodied in critical reviews and certain other noncommercial uses permitted by copyright law. For permission requests, write to the publisher, addressed "Attention: Permissions Coordinator," at the address below.

Indirect Knowledge Limited
2317 University Station
Murray, Kentucky/42071
www.indirectknowledge.com

Book Layout ©2014 Indirect Knowledge Limited

Ordering Information:
Quantity sales. Special discounts are available on quantity purchases by corporations, associations, and others. For details, contact the "Special Sales Department" at the address above.

The Sadhaka/ Bryan James Westra. —1st ed.
ISBN-10: 0990513203
ISBN-13: 978-0-9905132-0-9

Contents

A Poem [861] 5

"They say that "Time assuages" - Time never did assuage - An actual suffering strengthens As Sinews do, with Age - Time is a Test of Trouble - But not a Remedy - If such it prove, it prove too There was no Malady" 5

Moving Movers Can Be Moving 1

    The Mover Who Moved Me 5

The Girl at the Temple 15

    A Spiritual Girl, Indeed 16

    Sita's Apartment 20

Ryan Learns Hindi & Gets a New Name 29

    Lesson 1 32

    Lesson 2 41

    Lesson 3 52

Devotion, Obsession, or Control? 63

    Lesson 4 95

Lord's Park 119

Love 124

Lesson 5 131

ऐसा कहा जाता है 141

Lesson 6 144

सम्मोहित किया 159

Lesson 7 173

Decisions Decisions 197

Prema Talks to Sita 200

Dinner is Served with a Priceless Gift 205

भारत - मेरे घर 207

The Last Chapter 211

The Man I Call Sadhak & His Hindi Lessons 215

Dedicated to Jennifer A. Bonilla—You Are My Love Story!

A Poem [861]

"They say that "Time assuages" -
Time never did assuage -
An actual suffering strengthens
As Sinews do, with Age -

Time is a Test of Trouble -
But not a Remedy -
If such it prove, it prove too
There was no Malady"

— Emily Dickinson

CHAPTER 1

Moving Movers Can Be Moving

Now in my mind I was wounded; yet, what was to become of me, I did not know. I grew up sheltered, protected from the domains of dangers my parents knew growing up, a world I wasn't allowed to know existed, and I suppose I should thank them for it, but I'm not that sure I will.

Nineteen was the age that I'd become, quicklier than I noticed, and the death of my brother still impacted my mental health. My siblings and I had grown into individuals, losing our bond in the process of this evolution. Escaping to social groups that did not accept each other, and therefore we did not accept each other.

I, a spiritualist, my sister, a romanticist, my younger brother a recreationalist; we all had our outlets for dealing with the loss of our stepbrother. People grieve differently, though, what is interesting, is how people change in the process of grieving. I became different. They as well.

Had the death been natural, perhaps the depression would not have affected each of us as it had. Rowland, was exhausted, dealing with his own mother's death, whom I'll not speak of, and it was little wonder his choice of suicide was the exhaust pipe on his old Nissan truck, which was found eleven days later, in an old farmer's field, somewhere in Indiana. It was a closed casket funeral, and the mourner's were sick with the thoughts of the coroner's vivid recount of the body's condition, evertime one of them had inquired about why the funeral was closed casket. Perhaps it was a worse experience imaginging the condition of the body, than might have been the experience of actually seeing the body. I'm thankful though I did not see the body, because I could remember him, as he was, the last time I remember seeing him.

When three people have distinguished themselves as different, from one another, disagreements will naturally arise, and the three people will further grow farther apart. I don't blame them. The situation was what it was, and was not what it was not. No point in discussing it now, it won't change the past, nor heal the hurt; and by the time I recounted it, I would be changed and think, perhaps, differently—and, that, I don't want for myself or for them.

"We're nearly there guys," said my father.

"Where is there?" I asked him.

"Elgin, Nathan, Elgin."

His route had changed, and with change had to come more change; namely, a move from Bowling Green, Kentucky, to the west suburb of Chicago—Elgin, Illinios.

Bowling Green had been my home since first grade. We grew up on a four hundred and ninety acre horse farm in the countryside. We had lived in a log home, not to be mistaken for a log cabin, which my father had custom built to his specifications when I was twelve. I loved it there. I loved my horse Blacky, and would miss riding him bareback through our seven acre pond. I would miss the house, with the vaulted ceilings, and skylights. I would miss my friends, and miss my identity, which took me everbit of my life to build. Not much changes in Bowling Green. At least not in the rural area where I had lived.

When I was fifteen, I remember crying out to my Tennessee Walker, Blacky, my feelings about Roland's tragic and unexpected death. He was my best friend; a horse any introvert would have loved dearly. Animals listen better than humans, making them better friends. I will miss him very much.

"We're here you guys," shared my father, finally.

For nine hours he had endured highway hypnosis, as did we all, and it was nice to be anywhere, besides a packed car. Bodies touching bodies, bad breath and funky odors, and stale air, it was enough to make anyone despise their family members and want to rebel against moving. It sure didn't sell me on the move, any more than my father trying to convince me moving to Elgin would be an adventure. Some adventure!

"Is this our house," Michelle, my sister, asked.

"Yes, but this is a duplex. Our apartment is upstairs, we share the house. The apartment is spacious though.

You'll see," my father educated us, expecting there to be some conflict.

"I want to go back to Bowling Green. Dad, can we not stay here," Michelle expressed, distraughtly.

"Everyone listen up. This is our home now. We are not moving back to Bowling Green. Get that notion out of your heads. This is home now. Make the best of it. Do you all understand me?" said Dad.

Reluctantly everyone one of us indicated we understood.

Liberty street was not so liberating. The apartment was brown with beige trim. It was 1950s-ish. The yard was small, almost non-existent, and the houses were so close that it was uncomforting to know that others could watch you watching them as easily as they could expect you watching them watch you.

Inside the apartment were two bedrooms, a living area, a tiny bathroom, and a kitchen that separated the the two beds from the living room.

"Dad, seriously, there're are only two bedrooms. There're four of us. What were you thinking? I mean... really!" Michelle chastised.

"You'll take one of the bedrooms, Mitch and Ryan the other, and when I'm home, I'll sleep in the living room. It's doable, so just bare it. When you want to pay $2,000 a month in rent, we can get a bigger place. Until then, be grateful you have your own room.

Quit complaining! I'm sick of it!" voiced Dad.

That was all it took for each of us to grin and bare the situation. I was tired, the others were too, and I didn't have an argument in me. I was ready to find a comfortable place to lay my head, and leave the world behind as I dreamed dreams to dissociate myself as far away from this reality as I possibly could.

The Mover Who Moved Me

I awoke. It was the movers who woke me.

"Ryan, you're the only one still sleeping. It's time to meet the morning, and start stirring. Get up, please. The movers are here. I need your help directing them," said Dad.

"I'm getting up dad. Let me get dressed and I'll start directing," I said. I was disoriented, slightly not-all-there, and the last thing I wanted, truthfully, was to tell a bunch of movers, where everything went. Mainly, because I didn't know where to put everything. In fact, I didn't know where to put anything.

There were five movers and one large semi-truck parked at the road front. They were all in uniform. Three were under thirty, probably close to my age, and two were over forty, maybe even fifty. It was apparent who was running the show. It was man, wearing a long beard, who carried a gut, and looked like what I envisioned a Viking to look like. He had thick legs and arms, and a broad head. He was intimidating to me to look at. Thankfully he stayed in the trailer, pushing our furniture and belongings to the rear, where the underlings would get it and take it up the outside staircase and into our apartment.

The younger men got along well with each other. They clowned around a lot, but their strength and manpower was the force that moved the move along at a rapid pace. So much so that I had a difficult time thinking where to put things, because as soon as I thought about where to put one piece of furniture, they were bringing in another piece.

Dad was with Michelle and Mitch, down at the school, enrolling them in their sophomore year of high school. Dad didn't have time to mess around, because he was leaving out tonight to head for Minneapolis. Dad was a truck driver, though not the type to move furniture. He hauled for North American Van Lines, and was in their High Value Equipment division. Mostly what he hauled were large mainframe computers, expensive exercise equipment, and street sweepers. But, he hauled whatever his company contracted for him to haul, so it could be anything.

When the movers were finished, I was told I needed to go outside and sign the paperwork, and that would wrap things up.

I did just that, and finally made the acquaintance of the mystery man in the back of the trailer. His name, I learned, was Big Jack, at least that's what they called him.

"Everything where you want it?" Big Jack asked me.

"Yeah. Everything is exactly where it needs to be. You guys did a great job. Thanks for asking," I answered.

"What brought you to Chicago?" he asked me.

"My dad is a long haul truck driver, and his route has changed, so we moved here to accommodate that," I shared.

"Good profession. I've been a driver for 27 years," expressed Big Jake.

"Yeah. Dad's been doing it a long time. I don't know exactly how many years, but before I was born. So at least 19 years," I responded back.

"You're nineteen?" he asked me.

"Yes, Sir," I said.

"Need a job?" he offered.

"Yes. Actually, I need to start looking. I can't expect my dad to float the bill much longer," I said.

"I can get you a job as a lumper[1], helping me and my crew. If you're interested, give me a call tomorrow, about noon," he instructed me.

"I appreciate it. I will talk to my father, and I definitely will give you a call and let you know something. Thank you so much," I said excitedly.

"You're welcome. And, um, welcome to Chicago. Be seeing you now," Big Jake ended with, as he began walking back to the cab of his rig.

"A job. My first job. Maybe Chicago will be a good change of scenery. So far so good anyway," I thought, as I walked back up the staircase and entered the apartment.

I felt like I was being moved to do something responsible for once in my life. My father would be proud of me. Maybe I could save enough to buy a car.

Working toward a Goal

The next day made that call. I was given a job, and told to report to a warehouse in Addison. I learned quickly how to take the Metra Lines in Elgin, into the city, and from there, catch the L-Lines to Addison.

Baker's Warehouse was an agent of Belkin's National Moving & Storage. The agency took in freight and dispatched it out throughout the Chicagoland area and suburbs. The work was sometimes challenging, but I never complained. I took to the philosophy that if someone else could do it, so could I.

Big Jake was fair, but serious about doing an excellent job. There are no shortcuts he constantly reminded me. I often was made to stay later than the other guys on the crew, to help clean the warehouse, sweep out trailers, roll up cargo straps, and fold moving blankets called Pads[2].

One afternoon Big Jake, found me. I was folding and stacking pads. He said, "You're doing a fine job. Take a break," and then took a seat on the half pile I had started.

"Ryan, you've been here 11 months, and it's time you've gotten a raise. I'm giving you a dollar an hour more. You'll be making eleven dollars an hour now. Maybe this will help you be able to get that car you keep talking about wanting, a little sooner.

"You also get a ride home with Miles, here at five o'clock. He's agreed already to take you back over to Elgin.

"Anyway, that's all I wanted."

"Thank you sir," I told Big Jake. I wanted him to know I appreciated him helping me, and taking an interest in my work ethic. "I am deeply grateful for all you've done to help me, since I've moved to Elgin," I finished.

Big Jake just nodded, and left me to my work. At five o'clock I was given a ride back to Elgin, by my co-worker Miles.

Miles didn't strike me as all that intelligent, but he was a hard worker, and a very kind person. He would sometimes let me borrow money, between paychecks, when I needed it. He would give me rides home when he was going that way.

"I left my book back at the warehouse," I told Miles. We were nearly to my house.

"It will be there tomorrow," Miles assured me.

The book was, "Am I a Hindu," authored by Ed Vishwanathan. I had become attracted to this religion, Hinduism, since my brother's suicide. The knowledge was vast, and it was a challenge for me fully to wrap my mind around the many tenets of Hinduism. My family was not religious, but I found myself on a quest for truth, and wanted to believe there was more to life than some inevitable death; a fate all people meet eventually. Surely, I thought, there was more to life than some meaningless existence. The more I learned, the more I thirsted for knowledge, and the more I continued to learn.

Hinduism is a beautiful religion. It is all encompassing; that is to say, it is open to any belief or God or Goddess. It is embracing of anyone who chooses to accept it as their religion. It is the oldest living religion. Its holy books are the Vedas. These texts are many, and in truth one could never read them all in a single lifetime. The texts are written in Sanskrit. Sanskrit is considered by some a dead language; however, it is still spoken fluently in some small villages in India. Sanskrit, Hindus say, is the Language of God. The language is metered, and sung, and not spoken, in the sense that most languages are spoken. It is a hypnotic language; namely, sending people into trances and taking them into altered states of reality. No wonder, this language is a religious language, and one that reveals the great hidden mysteries of the truth of Hinduism.

"You're right. I'll just get it tomorrow. If you get there before me tomorrow, I left it on that stack of pads I was folding; can you pick it up and put it somewhere safe for me?" I asked Miles.

"Of course. I'll probably be one of the first people there. So I'll look for it as soon as I get in. I'll put in in your locker in the employee break area," said Miles.

When I entered the apartment, I was cold. The winter was harsh, and the winds were wickedly cold. People froze to death in these types of weathers. A bum was recently on the news, who had frozen to death, near the laundry mat, down from where I live. You have to be careful, if you're going to live here, because it only takes forgetting to prepare, and then you're doomed. Bowling Green never got this cold. The winds were never this iniquitous.

I turned on a heater, and another, and then wrapped myself in a blanket. Mitch was watching television. Michelle was in her room, doing something. Dad was on the road, I think in Salt Lake City, staying at a Ramada.

I needed quiet, so I went to mine and Mitch's room and took a book of my bookcase. It was the Bhagavada Gita[3]. I had just purchased it from Amazon.com. I started reading, and found myself lost in the pages, and by four o'clock in the morning, I had finished. I would never be the same, I reasoned to myself.

I didn't get much sleep, before I was awaken by my alarm clock. I was tired, weary, and losing patience with myself. I wish I had gotten more sleep, but I couldn't worry about that, because I had to catch the Metra.

I ran out of the house, and down to the station, and fortunately showed up right in time.

At work I was quiet. I had forgotten about leaving the book there, and so forgot to inquire of Miles about it. He never mentioned it either.

At five o'clock, I was the only one left, besides Big Jake. He met me at one of the trailers, holding the book. He asked me if I was interested in Hinduism, or if thought of myself as Hindu. I was shell-shocked with embarrassment. Most Caucasians are not Hindu, so I hated explaining my fascination and interest in Hinduism. I didn't want to be judged.

"Jake, when I was 15 my step-brother Roland, killed himself. My family isn't religious, and since his death I have been studying about world religions. When I came across Hinduism, something just felt right. I have been trying to learn more about the religion, but I haven't found much information about it," I admittedly revealed.

Jake just laughed at me. I was mortified. How can someone just laugh at another, when that person has just spilled their heart to you? How insensitive, I thought.

I guess my deer in the headlights look said enough, because he stopped laughing, and got more serious.

"Ryan, I'm not laughing at you. I'm laughing because I'm Hindu, and nobody here knows it. I go to temple off of Lunt Avenue every Sunday. You should come sometime. I'll pick you up if you like," said Big Jake.

Instantly, the social pressure to conform to another person's ideology evaporated. My fear and hesitation to say more, abated.

"When you say temple, do you mean a Hindu Temple?" I asked him.

"Yes. There's a Krishna Temple. We do Kirtan, and there's a vegetarian love feast, and you could meet a lot more Hindus," he said.

I had studied Krishna, all night long, as I read the Bhagavad Gita. I confessed that I had read it in an entire night, only the night before.

Jake, was on my level now, and he told me so many things I didn't know about Hinduism. I had a friend now instead of simply a boss.

He confided to me when he works, he looks at this work as worship to Lord Krishna. He explained his view of why it is so important to always be thinking of higher ideals and principles. He had a heart for Hinduism.

I couldn't believe, of all people in the world, that Big Jake was a Hindu. I was very likely as shocked to discover this, as he almost certainly was learning I too was Hindu.

Notes

[1] A lumper is someone who helps a truck driver, unload cargo, as well as helps them get backed into docks, and helps with miscellaneous tasks, not driving related.

[2] Pad is short for padding. Pads protect furniture from scrapes and damage while in transit to a destination to be off-loaded.

[3] The Bhagavad Gita literally translates to mean Song of God. It is, by some Hindus, considered the Hindu bible.

CHAPTER 2

The Girl at the Temple

The weeks passed. Then a month. Then a year. It was a year and not quite seven month since I had started going on Sundays with Big Jake to the Krishna temple in the Clark community. The temple was massive. High ceilings. Cathedral like, but actually an old Masonic Fraternity building, converted into a Krishna temple, years ago.

Then it happened...

I was 21, and she was 18. Her name was Sita. Like the Sita in Ramayana, she was beautiful, humble, and I was in love at first glance. I didn't even know her, oddly, but I knew I was very much in love.

It was the first time I had seen her there. I made it a point to welcome her, and she, seriously, looked at me, and said nothing. Somehow it made me like her more, but I can't explain the psychology behind this phenomenon.

"Namaste!" she said to me, upon exiting the program.

That was odd, I thought. She didn't acknowledge me, and when she left, I was the only one she acknowledged.

"Namaste![1]" I returned, with a smile. I wished she'd said more, but that single expression of acknowledgement made me feel elated, and on cloud nine. Funny, how little things can be so meaningful. Paradoxical how less is sometimes more.

I now had a car. The car was old, but the car was new, to me, and I had saved up the money all on my own to buy it. I had saved $2,900 and paid it off in cash. It freed me up to experience more of the city. It allowed me to leave work when I wanted to. It was nice, and I didn't take it for granted. I was very appreciative of my blue Corolla. It was a dependable car, and the heat worked fantastically.

I was driving back to Elgin, that night, thinking about the girl at the temple; wondering if I would ever see her again. Before I knew it I was in the driveway, walking up the staircase, and oblivious to how I'd gotten there. My mind was busy, focused on the Girl; not on the drive or the conscious activities I was subconsciously engaged in at this point in time. I was hypnotized by love.

A Spiritual Girl, Indeed

I came under the spell of religion, the mythology, the culture of Hindus, and I assimilated myself with all of this in my mind, and deeds. I began praying each morning, at my makeshift mandir[2], and regularly read the Vedas, Upanishads, and spiritual epics Mahabharata and Ramayana.

The habit of associating with one's beliefs is reinforcing and spiritually uplifting. I was achieving an identity, which I felt right about. I'm not sure how explain this logically, yet, people who have a desire for something, willing to sacrifice for something beyond their own selfish desires, might understand on some level, what I'm saying.

The principles of Hinduism suited me. I slowly integrated as a Hindu, yet the more I involved myself, the more I felt religious and spiritual. This made me feel close to God. I was on the path of moksha[3]. Having a goal and direction was liberating in itself, lending me a sense of purpose.

"What is your name?" she asked me, finding me pacing up and down the back alley of the temple. It was Tuesday. I sometimes, on my days off, visited the temple, because I had nothing else to do, and also because I enjoyed the vibe of the place, and because in the basement was a restaurant named Govinda's, which served delicious Indian vegetarian fare.

"I'm Ryan," I shared.

"I mean your Hindu name?" she inquired.

"I don't have one," I admitted to her.

"Why?" she asked me.

"I don't know. I don't know how to get one. What's yours?" I stated and asked her.

"I'm Sita."

"Sita. That's beautiful," I told her.

She smiled at me, but I somehow didn't think it was because she was impressed with my compliment. Maybe she found me odd. I felt odd around her; as maybe though

I was not significant enough, or knowledgeable enough to associate with her. I was intrigued by her mystery, and wanted to know her better. Who was she anyway?

"I haven't seen you at the temple before. Are you new to the area?" I asked her.

"I just moved here from Saint Louis," she stated.

"I've not been here quite two years, myself. I moved from Bowling Green, Kentucky," I shared without her asking me. "What are you doing here?" I asked.

"I'm here to pray, and learn Hindi," she revealed to me.

"Hindi?" I questioned her.

"I'm moving to India, eventually. I am learning Hindi, to be able to communicate more effectively." She said.

"Why are you moving to India?" I asked.

"It's the Motherland of Hinduism, and where I belong," she said.

Sita was pale white. Skinny. Taller than her age. She had dark almond, almost black, hair. She wore it in a ponytail. When she walked it bounced. It gave her a carefree look, which matched her spirit. She always wore a sari, looking very Hindu. Between her eyebrows, slightly higher, was a red bindi[4] she wore. Eighteen, she was young, yet she represented herself by carrying herself as older and more mature. My impression of her was that she was very intelligent, with a higher than average I.Q.

"So you're just going to go to India?" I questioned her.

"Eventually, yes," she said emphatically.

"It is cold outside here. Do you want to take darshana[5] and then go for prasadama[6]?" she asked me.

"Yes," I replied.

Together we entered the temple, and I followed her toward the murtis[7]. I followed her lead. When she prayed, it was very authentic and a sensation came over me which alerted me to the fact that she was a very devout Hindu girl. The significance of her devotion, made me humble and more devoted myself. I had a spiritual experience in her presence.

After praying she led me down to the basement, and at the buffet, asked me if I liked Indian pickle. I had never had any, but told her yes, to seem more knowledgeable and Hindu than I actually was. She served me a small amount on my plate, standing next to me. The food looked very appetizing, though I didn't know what most of the dishes were. I simply took a little of everything, hoping I liked it all.

When we sat, I started to eat, but she stopped me and told me to pray. I did.

"Are you going to eat Indian style?" she asked me.

"You're joking, right?" I asked. I had no idea what she meant.

"No," she answered. She looked at me the way a manager might look at an employee, who was questioning their instructions. She was very serious looking.

"What's Indian style?" I questioned her.

"Eating with your hand," she replied.

I was flabbergasted speechless.

"Wash your hands with me," she instructed.

We walked to a corner of Govinda's where a small wash basin was located, and washed our hands. Then we returned to our table.

"Like this," she showed me.

It was a new experience.

After we ate, she took out a Ziploc bag from her purse, and pulled out some Hindi flashcards. She began studying the cards, and I just watched her, entrancedly.

"Ryan, what type of work do you do?" she asked me, randomly. Taking me by surprise.

"I work as a lumper for a trucking company in Addison," I told her.

"Do you have to work tomorrow?"

"No. I'm off. I don't go back until Friday," I shared.

"Do you want to get out of here?" she asked.

"Sure. We can," I said.

"We can go to my place," she suggested.

"Okay. Sure," I said.

She stood up first. I followed behind. I followed her outside, back to the alleyway.

"We can take my car. I'll drop you back tomorrow," she said.

I was nervous. I don't know why. I didn't know what was expected of me I suppose. I had been agreeable all night long, and now was going to be no different.

"Sure, that'll work," I agreed.

Sita's Apartment

Sita's apartment was a short ways away from the temple. She lived by herself. The complex, was a pale pinkish-brown, run-down looking, building. There were broken windows in some of the apartments from the outside of the building, I noticed upon first observation. There were old vehicles, and the place was eerie with men standing outside, drinking beers, and smoking cigarettes. It didn't look like any place an eighteen year old girl belonged, especially a religious girl with good values. It didn't seem to bother her though. She seemed quite acquainted with the place, and comfortable. More comfortable than me.

When we got to the front of the building, it dawned on me that it was an old motel that had been run into the ground, and was now a cheap apartment complex, with poor management.

The metal staircase, was not the safest thing in the world. It shook a little as we climbed the steps. When we got to the third story, she made a right and walked seven or eight doors down, and said, "This one's mine," and smiled at me.

I tried to smile back, but only nodded my head yes, hearteningly. Inside, there was no furniture. There were clothes strung on a clothesline inside the front room. There was a small wooden temple about two feet high sitting in one corner, with a Goddess murti placed on it. There was a small oil lamp to the right of the temple, and a small bookshelf, next to that, containing a small collection of Hindu spiritual texts. I couldn't make out what they were, because they were authored in Sanskrit or Hindi and written in Devanagari[8].

Sita walked to the other side of the room, where I noticed was a stove, refrigerator, sink, and some counter space. It was an efficiency apartment she lived in. Very small.

"Please take your shoes off," she requested. She had already slipped hers off, and placed them by the front entrance.

I complied.

"Just like at the mandir, eh?" I questioningly commented.

"Just like the mandir," she assured with conviction.

"Ryan, do you want some water?" she offered me.

"Sure," I said. There's something comforting about holding a glass, when you're in a strange new environment, in which you're unsure of how to behave, what to say, or how to respond. It was awkward. I felt awkward. Like a fish out of water.

"Here," she said, handing me the glass.

"Thanks," I replied. Thanks is universal. Can't go wrong saying thank you.

"So this is your place?" I asked.

"Yeah. Been here about a month now. It's nice having my own place," she said.

"What about your family?" I questioned.

"They're back in Saint Louis," she said.

For a couple hours we talked. We even laughed, if you can believe it. I really like this girl, I thought. She was strong mentally, and self-assured. I actually envied her for it, because I realized straightaway she was stronger than me. More grown-up anyway.

Since there wasn't a bedroom, we both slept on the floor, but on separate pallets[9]. I was respectful with my thoughts, though part of me wished I was sleeping next to her. Holding her. It was a fantasy I had.

At three o'clock in the morning, her alarm went off, and she woke, and took a shower. She then woke me, and let me take a shower also. I didn't know what time it was. I only knew it was dark outside, and there was a lot less traffic outside her apartment. I assumed it was seven o'clock for some reason. Don't know why though. I expected it to be later than it was, I guess.

Seriously, who gets up at three o'clock?

After I showered, I put back on my clothes and met her back in the front room.

"You're wearing your same clothes? I put a dhoti[10] on the shelf for you, and a kurta[11]. Are you not going to wear them?" she asked.

"I didn't know they were for me," I confessed to her.

"How do I wear them?" I questioned.

"Bring them here, I'll show you," she instructed.

I went back into the bathroom, found them, and brought them back to her.

"Take off your pants and shirt," she said.

"Seriously?" I asked, embarrassed.

"Don't be embarrassed Ryan. Just do it," she commanded me.

I complied, hesitatingly. I first took off my shirt, a polo, and then took off my blue jeans. I was shivering, and my body produced goose bumps. The nipples on my chest hardened. I was shaking, it was so cold.

Sita dressed me, like a mother dresses a small child. She started with the dhoti, and pleated it, tucked it, and wrapped and draped it, and I was totally lost as to how she did it, but the dhoti was finally finished. Then she took the Kurta out of a plastic bag, and unfolded it, and helped me get it on, pulling it down in the back, and sure enough it fit perfectly.

Before we left the house, she reached in a cabinet, above the stove, and pulled out a masala dabla[12], and sprinkled some dried turmeric in a smaller container, and added some lemon juice, from a fresh lemon. The saffron colored turmeric turned a bright red color.

"This is kunkumam[13], Ryan. You wear it between your eyes. It is a sacred mark. Lean down, so I can apply it to your forehead," she instructed me.

I complied.

After applying a red dot to my forehead, she applied one to herself.

"Come let's worship, before we go to temple," she insisted.

We walked over to her temple, sat on the floor Indian style. She pulled from her bookshelf a Sanskrit text named the *Lalita Sahasranama Stotram*[14]. She began reciting, and I listened. After which we said prayers, and she performed a puja[15] to honor the Divine Goddess Lalitambika.

"Ryan, it is time to leave for temple. Come," she directed me.

I complied.

It was nearing four-thirty when Sita and Ryan arrived at the temple. They parked alongside Ryan's Corolla. Together they walked into the temple, and joined the other devotees. They worshiped, did kirtan[16], prayed and did japa[17], nearly all morning, until it was time to take prasadam in Govinda's.

The day was much more devout than Ryan was accustomed to. He was feeling much more part of the Hindu fold, being with Sita.

Notes

[1] Namaste literally means I worship the God in you, which is a mirror image of myself. It is a Sanskrit term, used as a greeting or goodbye among Hindus.

[2] Mandir is synonymous for temple, and Hindus often will have a small temple in their homes, signifying their devotion to a particular Hindu deity.

[3] Moksha is the Hindu concept of liberation. It is a Sanskrit term, closely identifiable with the Buddhist concept of Nirvana.

[4] Bindi, is a mark worn by both Hindu men and women to represent their third eye, or sixth sense, which was a mark of devotion.

[5] Darshana, is a prayerful worship done in front of the deities.

[6] Prasadama, is sanctified food, which has been offered as an offering to the deities and then distributed to the devotees. It is a symbolic act of God providing for our needs and sustenance.

[7] Murtis are the deities or idols on display at a Hindu temple. They are the representation of Gods and Goddesses which preside over that temple, which devotees worship.

[8] Devanagari is the script that Sanskrit, Hindi, Marathi, and some other Indian languages are written in.

[9] Pallets are make-shift beds, in which blankets are layered on a floor, and slept on, without a mattress or traditional bed.

[10] Dhoti is a long piece of fabric, which is draped around a man's waistline and legs, worn as pants. It is a traditional Hindu garment.

[11] Kurta is an Indian shirt that is worn with a dhoti. It is a traditional Indian garment.

[12] Masala Dabla is a spice box, which is common in Hindu kitchens. It contains common spices used to prepare Indian food.

[13] Kunkumam is a red paste made of turmeric and lime or lemon juice, worn between the eyes of Hindu devotees and sadhaks.

[14] *Lalita Sahasranama Stotram* is a thousand mantra compilation of names of the Divine Goddess Lalitambika.

[15] Puja is a ritualistic worship ceremony to honor and bestow love and devotion on a god of goddess in the Hindu pantheon.

[16] Kirtan is devotional dancing.

[17] Japa is recitation of mantras on a Hindu rosary of 108 Tulsi or Sandalwood beeds.

CHAPTER 3

Ryan Learns Hindi & Gets a New Name

I heard it once said, by a pastor, "When two people meet, and make association with one another; one will conform to the other or the other to the one," and I find this to be true in this story. You see Ryan and Sita became friends. Ryan admired Sita's devotion, her knowledge of the religion he loved, and certainly, her. Sita, well, now there's a mysterious girl. She was simple. Her life regulated. She had something internally inside of her beyond the scope of what most might understand who've grown up in a western, American values, society. She was a true believer type. She embraced Hinduism, Hindu culture, and when push came to shove, believed she was just as Indian as any other Indian Hindu on the planet. She truly felt it her dharma[1] to be in India; specifically, fulfilling the role of a Hindu wife, active in that role, and, well, it was all in her imagination.

When the imagination and will are in conflict, as expressed by Emile Coue's Law of Reversed Effort, the imagination invariably always wins. Imagination is more powerful than willpower, and try as you might, you'll always fail to get what you want, if it is not aligned with your imagination. Likewise be careful what you imagine, you may very well get what you don't want. Everything in existence was first a thought in the mind of some being or god. The impossible becomes impossible if you believe it. The possible becomes possible if you believe it.

A few months passed. Ryan fell under Sita's alluring mystery, and lack of revealing anything about her family, her past, or much besides Hinduism and her Hindi lessons. The more time Ryan spent with her, the more he fell under love's spell. His heart, it was committed to her. Ryan was becoming more and more attached to Sita.

Sita on the other hand, she kept her safeguards and her heart protected, yet she cared deeply for Ryan. She was confused however about her feelings for him. Regardless of how much she cared for him, she was dedicated to the mission of following out her dharma. Ryan didn't know how or to what extent Sita would go or what she would give up to succeed in living her dharma. He would learn.

"Sita, I am getting my Hindu name, tonight. My namakarana samskara[2] is at five-thirty. Please say you'll be there," Ryan excitedly relayed to Sita.

"Ryan, I will be there. I am soooo happy for you," said Sita.

At five-thirty Ryan, became Saratchandra; meaning, autumn moon. He was in a state of blessedness, after receiving his name. He received this name, in particular, because it was the Hindu month of Kartika and the first day of the month long Damodara festival, and Sharad-Purnima festival, which is significant to Hindus, because it's the first night of Lord Krishna's Rasa dance, and it's a very auspicious month for practicing bhakti-yoga[3]. To be given this name, now, was very auspicious for the former Ryan.

"Saratchandra, is very auspicious," relayed Sita to him.

"I cannot explain how I feel at this moment Sita."

"You need not. I know how you feel," said Sita to him.

After the ceremony, devotees celebrated Damodara by lighting ghee lamps, and everyone wore white, to reflect the moon. It was a very special-special, night. Hypnotic to say the least.

Saratchandra spent the night at Sita's and awoke with her the next morning, something he had been doing a lot lately. Spending time with her, made him feel more spiritual and religious. He was integrating more and more fully into the Hindu fold. Now he had a name that reflected his devotion and commitment to his new religion.

Induction takes time. When done slowly enough, one does not know one is transitioning, adopting the culture, and the person one becomes holistically, goes undetected, and surpasses a person's critical faculty. One just becomes oneself by ones' devotion to ones' beliefs.

Love is a language that is immortal. It is embedded in the language of God; a language forgotten and lost in a language many have said is dead. When you open yourself to the expansion of knowledge, you open yourself to a new world—not a dead world.

When you fall in love, the world stands still, and your imagination becomes focused on what you truly desire and wish to know, and alchemy happens. This is the state of mind required to learn anything important to you. When you fall in love with someone, that person is more important than anything else, and everything you do is a result of that love. Your beliefs about love influence your love, your ability to love, and how others love you. For this reason it is recommended to get your beliefs in check to achieve the outcomes you desire most.

Lesson 1.

"Saratchandra it is time to awaken," Sita said to him. Saratchandra was sleeping peacefully, not wanting to awaken, and refused.

"Wake-up Saratchandra, it is time for temple," Sita said again, nudging him.

"I'm up! I'm up! Sita, I was having the most amazing dream," Saratchandra said.

"What was it about?" Sita inquired.

"It was about..." Rasa hesitated.

"Yes?" Sita said.

"Hmm I have forgotten it now. I remember it was good, though," Saratchandra said to her.

"Well, get a shower. I already have taken mine. Time is fleeting. Don't take too long. Okay?" She said.

"Right, I'll only be a few minutes," Saratchandra said, standing to his feet, and heading toward Sita's bathroom.

A few minutes later he came out dhoti clad, and ready to worship with her.

Like usual Sita recited *Rahasya Namah Sahasra*[4], and then the two of them prayed, and Sita performed a Puja to Devi[5].

After this, Sita drove them in her old blue Chevy Celebrity, back to the temple, so they could take part in the morning program.

After the program was finished, Saratchandra drove to work.

"Did you get all those pads folded, and the straps rolled," Big Jake asked Saratchandra.

"Yes sir. All of them," said Saratchandra.

"Well, I guess you can get out of here. I appreciated your help today, over in Kankakee, you almost could handle a crew all by yourself. Maybe there's a promotion for you soon, if you keep performing at the level you have been lately.

"How's everything going anyhow?" asked Big Jake.

"Everything is fine. Everything is awesome," Saratchandra said, emphasizing the word awesome. Big Jake noticed, Saratchandra was behaving like a young man in love, but didn't interfere, since his love life wasn't seemingly interfering with his work.

At five o'clock, Saratchandra entered Govinda's, where he knew he would find Sita.

"Namaste Sita!"

"Namaste Saratchandra ji," she returned.

"What are you up to?" he asked her.

"Studying my Hindi, like always," she said.

"Sita, is Hindi difficult to learn?" Saratchandra inquired of her.

"No, Saratchandra, Hindi is an easy language to learn. It's phonetic, and if you can pronounce the alphabet, it is easy to learn the words required to communicate with people on an interpersonal level.

"Hindi is the national language of India.

"Do you want me to teach you?" Sita asked Saratchandra.

Now, Saratchandra was not really an academic, and the thought of learning a new language, he thought would be too difficult for him. Remember, though, back to what I said earlier, regarding Coue's Law.

Saratchandra's will was to learn Hindi; however, in his imagination it was an impossibility. This meant he would fail should he attempt to learn the foreign language. Until he believed it was easy, it would be difficult, if not impossible for him to learn.

"I do want to learn, but I don't think I can. I tried learning French in high school, but I wound up failing. Then I tried Spanish, and again failed. Me and languages—don't mix," confessed Saratchandra.

"I see. I cannot teach you Hindi then," Sita said.

"I thought you could teach anything?" Saratchandra jested.

"I can. But you have failed before starting, and so what's the point?" she asked, with sadness and upset in her voice.

She began packing up her learning materials, and left, without saying another word.

"Where are you going? Why are you upset?" Saratchandra pleaded with her, but she just kept walking, ignoring his pleas.

"Sita!...Sita!!...Sita!!!" he cried out, louder and louder, confused, but wanting her not to go.

"Now I'm upset," Saratchandra thought to himself. He decided to go for a walk through the alley way, down some other side streets, and eventually made his way down to the beach.

The beach, was quiet. There weren't many people there. Only wandering wonderers, like Saratchandra, lost in thoughts, and confusion. Filled with emotions they couldn't understood, because they had never experienced them before.

"You only appreciate happiness, when you experience sadness.

"What did I do to upset her?

"Why is she mad at me?

"How can I fix this?

"Should I go after her, or let her blow off some steam?

"Girls are confusing," all these thoughts raced through his mind.

"Why does he not get it?" Sita thought to herself, thinking about Saratchandra's self-defeating attitude.

"Why does he let his thoughts limit him?

"Doesn't he know this is important to me and should be to him?" she thought, not able to focus anymore on her Hindi lesson.

"Knock, knock, knock, anybody there?" said Saratchandra, standing in the doorway of Sita's apartment. He was peaking in through the front door, watching Sita, watch him be foolish. He saw her crying.

"Don't cry Sita. Please don't cry. Can I come in?" Saratchandra asked implored her.

"No jerks allowed," she said.

"Sita, please. I want to learn Hindi. I can learn it. I'll take it seriously, I promise," he said convincingly.

"Promise?" she asked him.

"I promise. I promise you. Please let me come in," Saratchandra requested.

Sita stood to her feet, and walked to the glass storm door, where Saratchandra had his face pressed against the glass.

"Okay. But first, you have to promise me you'll not be a defeatist. I will teach you, but you have to know that you are capable of learning. It is the only way. Do you promise?" she asked him.

"Sita. I promise I will learn. I won't let a few negative experiences keep me from succeeding. I promise you'll I'll study hard, and take everything you tell me seriously. I want to learn. Come-on please teach me. Please. Pretty please Sita," said Saratchandra.

Sita opened the door, and let him in.

"Today, I will teach you the alphabet, and the Devanagari script. This will be your first lesson. If you're ready, we can begin," she said.

"I'm ready to learn," Saratchandra said.

"Come and sit down on the floor. I'll grab a notebook, and we can start the lesson," said Sita.

The Devanagari Script & Hindi Alphabet

"First I will teach you the vowels. Remember, each letter has a sound. Only one sound. If you learn how each letter sounds, you'll be able to read any word, correctly, which you experience through your sense of sight. You can listen to a word, and likewise see how it is spelled in your mind, and be able to write it correctly, because how it sounds is how it is written. Do you understand?" Sita asked Saratchandra.

"Yes. Each letter has a sound. If I see a word spelled I will be able to pronounce it. If I hear a word spoken, I will be able to write it. That's awesome!" commented Saratchandra.

"I told you learning Hindi is easy," she rubbed in.

"Okay, funny, I deserve that, but how do you write and pronounce these vowels?"

"Well, let me show you." With that said, Sita began writing out all the vowels in Devanagari with the roman script counterpart, next to each of the vowels, as each character would be pronounced in English, so Saratchandra could understand and practice.

Independent Vowel Characters

अ *a*	आ *aa*	इ *ĭ*	ई *ēē*
उ *uh*	ऊ *oo*	ऋ *r̥hĭ*	
ए *ē*	ऐ *aī*	ओ *ō*	औ *au*

"Saratchandra, do you see these vowels?" asked Sita to him.

"Yes, I see them. But how do you pronounce them?" Saratchandra asked her.

"Okay, pay attention, and I will explain.

"The first vowel is अ and is pronounced like the short 'u' sound in the word 'cup'.

"So say the word '**u**p' without the 'p' on the end," instructed Sita.

"uh," said Saratchandra.

"Very good. You have pronounced it correctly. Now for the next vowel आ.

"This vowel is the sound you make when a doctor puts a tongue depressor in your mouth and asks you to say **ahhh**. It is the same vowel sound in mop. Like you're going to m**o**p up the floor. Now say it aloud," Sita instructed.

"aah" pronounced Saratchandra.

"Very good. You are learning nicely. Now for the next vowel इ.

"This vowel makes the same sound as the shortened i sound in the English alphabet. It is the i-sound in the word 'it' without the 't' added. Now pronounce 'it,' without the 't' added onto the end.

"ihh," pronounced Saratchandra.

"Again you did a remarkable job pronouncing it. Your Hindi Saratchandra is coming along very nicely. Let's try another. This time the vowel ई.

"This vowel is pronounced 'e' as in 'kēy' or 'swēēt.' It is the long 'ēē' sound in the English alphabet. Pronounce it now," insisted Sita.

"ēēēē," said Saratchandra.

"Remarkable job!" she praised him.

"Now the next vowel उ.

"This vowel makes the same sound as the double o's in the word 'foot' or 'cook' or the single 'u' in 'put.'

"Can you pronounce it?"

"Sure, 'oo,'" repeated Saratchandra.

"Now the next vowel ऊ makes the sound of double 'oo' also, but it is elongated, and stretched, and sounds like the 'oo' in 'pool,' or 'food.'

"Pronounce it, please, Surtachandra" Sita pressed for.

"oooo" Saratchandra pronounced, correctly.

"Now Saratchandra, the next vowel is ऋ, and sounds like the noise a piece of paper makes when we rip it. It is pronounced '–ṛi' as in 'rip' or 'script,'" she instructed him.

"Say it please," commanded Sita, proud her student was learning so quickly.

"iīī," pronounced Surtachandra.

"Nice job. Now for another.

"The next vowel is ए and it makes the long ā sound in English. It is how the vowel 'a' sounds said when saying the word hāte or māte or lāte.

"Pronounce this sound for me Saratchandra," requested Sita.

"āāāā" he said.

"Nice here's another vowel. It is ऐ, and it is pronounced like the long ī in English. You can think of the sentence: "I am going," and remember it's the first word "I" that is this letter in Devanagari.

"Okay, you know the drill. Pronounce it," said Sita.

"I" said Saratchandra.

"Easy eh?" asked Sita.

"Easy!" returned Saratchandra.

"Just two more, to go. The first is ओ, and it is pronounced like the long 'ō' sound. It is the 'ō' in 'home.' Say it for me, so I know you understand," said Sita.

"ō," said Saratchandra.

"The last one is औ, and it is the sound you make when someone pinches you. **Owww!!** You can also think of it as 'ar' when you say the word '**car**' if that makes it easier for you to remember.

"So Saratchandra, you have been given an explanation of the Hindi vowels. Now it is time for you to practice.

"Just so you know. Until you learn the Devanagari alphabet, you will not be permitted to learn any words. A Hindu should be able to both read, write, and pronounce the Devanagari alphabet. Too many books teach Hindi through roman script, and this is not, in my opinion the best way to learn. However, it is useful to learn the pronunciation of the characters, until you make that transition to Hindi inflection on words.

"Now practice, and I will teach you the consonants. The ball is in your court. It is up to you to prove your devotion to learning. If you do not have these vowels memorized, able to write them fluently, and say them correctly, without thinking about it, I will not teach you the consonants.

"I am not doing this to be mean; only doing it to ensure you are ready to move on. Everybody learns at a different pace. The more you practice, the more you'll achieve, and faster. It really is that simple.

"See I told you learning Hindi is simple," said Sita to Saratchandra.

"Sita, you are a good teacher. I will practice, practice, practice. Thank you for the lesson," expressed Saratchandra to her thankfully.

"You're welcome. Now I'll leave you alone for some hours to let you practice," she said, standing up, and walking over to another corner, where she began practicing her own advanced level Hindi lesson.

Lesson 2

"Sita, I have them memorized," said Saratchandra, confidently and excitedly.

"Can you pronounce them, and write them?" she asked.

"Yes. I can. I can do both; write and pronounce them.

"You'll have to prove it to me, before I give you another lesson."

Saratchandra wrote each letter, in order, and after writing each one, pronounced its sound. He didn't make a mistake.

"Now let me write one, and you pronounce it," Sita insisted.

Rasa messed up. He had memorize them in order, and therefore memorized the pronunciations, through this association. When he was presented with a vowel, at random, it was much more challenging, and he didn't remember what it sounded like.

Sita pulled out some flashcards, which she had purchased, online, many months earlier, at: www.indirectknowledge.com. They were the vowel letters on one side, and the pronunciation and an example on the reverse side. She mixed them up, and handed them to Saratchandra.

Saratchandra looked at the deck of flashcards, and then back at Sita, and huffed, knowing it was going to be more challenging than he first thought. He wanted to impress her, but she wanted him to learn correctly.

"Saratchandra, don't look so dejected. You are learning. You are doing a fine job. Your dedication to learning is impressive. Now, practice with these flashcards, until the vowels become ingrained in your brain. Learning is an unconscious process, and you are learning, even when you don't think you are learning. Keep practicing," she encouraged him.

Saratchandra, was humbled. Learning is a humbling process. That humility brings us closer to God. Saratchandra was learning more than just Hindi. He was learning a lesson in devotion and self-effacement.

The rest of the night was spent studying his Hindi. When he wanted to give up, he looked up and would find Sita still studying her flashcards devotedly, and this would encourage him to persist in his studies. Eventually, he fell into a learning trance. When you fall into a learning trance, you are learning at the deepest level of unconscious learning, where your Other Mind [6]is absorbing and helping you learn everything, even when your Mind[7] isn't functioning in the way that you think it should.

The next morning, Sita awoke Saratchandra, and bade him to get ready. It was time to greet the new day.

In the shower, Saratchandra was seeing the Devanagari characters in his mind, and could hear the sounds of each letter in his mind. He had learnt them.

Upon this realization he started crying. He couldn't believe it. It is an emotionally spiritual experience when you have achieved a goal; namely, after you have learnt something you didn't at first feel confident in learning.

God helps you learn, when you trust God to help you. You only have to be devoted to the action of learning, surrendering it over to God through extreme devotion, for the intercessory power of God to take effect and you will be affected emotionally. You will.

After Sita chanted Lalita Sahasranama, and they prayed, and sang some bhajans[8], she drove them to the temple, and they both participated in the morning program and did mangal aroti[9], and chanted the Maha Mantra, until it was time to eat morning prasadam.

After the worship, Saratchandra left for work, and Sita left for her home, to clean up the residence, do her and Saratchandra's laundry, and to wait until it was time to meet Saratchandra back at the temple at five-thirty.

"I have good news for you," said Big Jake to Saratchandra.

"Yeah? What is it?" he asked.

"You're being promoted to warehouse manager. You'll now receive a salary, instead of an hourly wage. They're giving you $45,000 per year. You'll still only be required to work 40 hours per week. Your checks will more than double," said Big Jake.

"Oh my goodness. That's wonderful. I cannot believe it. Why, did they select me, do you think?" asked Saratchandra.

"Your work ethic. They higher-ups have noticed your dedication to your work. See why I pushed you this whole time to perform your work as an offering to God. It is a blessing from Lord Krishna, which has brought you this boon. You should surely say a prayer of thanks.

"I am so proud of you. I know you will do an excellent job.

"You'll find out about it this afternoon, when you're called in to the office. Act surprised, will yah?" asked Big Jake.

"I most surely will. I am utterly shocked. I cannot believe they selected me out of everyone else. Sita will be happy too. I am so happy. I just want to do a good job, and make you all proud of me Big Jake," admitted Saratchandra.

"You won't have a problem with accomplishing that. We already have faith in your abilities, because you have faith in your abilities. When you know you can do something, it doesn't matter what others tell you, because knowing is more valuable than simply the desire to do something. With knowing comes confidence and ability. You have proven your abilities here. You know you are going to be capable of producing good results. This is why you most likely were designated for the promotion of warehouse manager.

"Anyway, I have to get back to work. I'm taking a crew of guys up to Milwaukee for a move. I won't return back here until sometime tomorrow night. Anyway, I just wanted to be the first to share the news with you.

"Take care of yourself Saratchandra. Make us proud!" said Big Jake.

"I will and thanks. I'll see you in a day or so. Be careful driving up there," said Saratchandra to him.

It was probably the easiest day Saratchandra had worked for the company. When your mind is in one place, and your body in another, everything you're doing goes unnoticed and not minded. Saratchandra could not stop thinking about his promotion. At the end of the day, around four-thirty, he was called into the dispatch office, where he was given his promotion.

Like he promised Big Jake, he would; he acted completely shocked, and totally thrilled by the news. It was like a surprise birthday party had just been showered on him, and he was oblivious to the fact it was his birthday. This is how he responded by the promotion being given to him.

At five o'clock Saratchandra left Addison, and headed to the temple. On the way, he was mapping out in his mind, exactly how he would share the good news with Sita. He wanted it to be perfect.

"Saratchandra, it is five-thirty, it is time to take darshana and prasadam, yes?" Sita asked him.

"Yes," he replied, "But, I want to..."

"Come, you can tell me later, it's time now," she pushed, interrupting him from revealing the good news.

After prayer and food, Sita didn't give him a chance to express his excitement or the good news. She pulled out a piece of paper, and told him to write the vowels, and pronounce them.

After he had done that, she took out the vowel flashcards, mixed them up, and flashed them before him and made his recite the sound each one made. Instantly, Saratchandra forgot about his promotion, and began zeroing in on the lesson. He wanted to be able to move on to the second lesson, but knew Sita would not let that happen until he had accomplished the first one masterfully.

"Very good Saratchandra. Very good. You have done as you promised me and learnt the first lesson well. Now, today, I will give you lesson two—Devanagari consonants. Are you ready?" she asked him.

"I'm ready," said Saratchandra.

"Here are the consonants. They are many; however, there is a trick to learning them. Let me show you, and then I'll explain the trick that makes it easy to learn them by memory" said Sita.

On that note, she took her notebook and began writing out the Devanagari consonants and their roman script counterparts.

Devanagari Hindi Consonants

क ka ख kha ग ga घ gha ङ ang

च cha छ chha ज ja झ jha ञ nya

ट ṭa ठ ṭha ड ḓa ढ ḓha ण rṇa

त ta थ tha द da ध dha न na

प pa फ pha ब ba भ bha म ma

य ya र ra ल la ळ lla व va

श sha ष sha स sa ह ha

क्ष ksha त्र tra ज्ञ jnya श्र shra

ज़ za ड़ r(a ढ़ r(ha फ़ fa

० abbreviation marker

Saratchandra's eyes glazed over as Sita wrote out the various letters. He was thinking it would take forever to learn this alphabet thing. He found himself defeating himself before even giving himself a chance to learn. This is why many students of a foreign language give up.

Ironically, what most students do not realize is how there are so few difficult parts, and so many more easy parts. It is really is easy to get over the difficult humps, and be able to learn the easy parts effortlessly. That's what is needed, mindset wise, to learn a language.

"Now, for the trick. Saratchandra, the trick here is to think about where your tongue is positioned in your mouth when you say these letters aloud. The Devanagari characters were formed around sounds being uttered out of the speaker's mouth.

"Think of a set as being a line. You read left to right each set. Notice that the first set; viz.: क *ka* ख *kha* ग *ga* घ *gha* ङ *ang* are formed more toward the back of the mouth. The क *ka* sound is very much the same position in the mouth one might be when reciting the word candy. It sounds the same, actually. For this first set, you stay at this location. Linguistically speaking, this location of syllabary is referred to as the Velar position. Velar sounds are produced in the throat of the mouth.

"In Hindi there are some sounds that are more aspirated than others. This distinguishes some of the letters from others. For example, the letter क *ka* is unaspirated, while the letter ख *kha* is aspirated. The term aspiration refers to how much air comes after the letter. So how you distinguish क *ka* from ख *kha* is by the 'ha' part which is an intentional quick exertion of breath that sets the difference between the two syllables.

"The next set; namely: च *cha* छ *chha* ज *ja* झ *jha* ञ *nya* are produced slightly further and more towards the front of the mouth. If you say, 'Choo Choo Train' the 'Ch' on 'Choo Choo' is about where you want to be when you pronounce this set of syllables. Notice that your tongue cannot help but touch the palatal part of the mouth; and, in fact, this is the linguistic term, used to identify this set of characters, i.e. Palatal.

"The next set; namely: ट *ṭa* ठ *ṭha* ड *ḍa* ढ *ḍha* ण *ṛa* require the tongue to curl back to touch the palate. These sounds are 'hard' sounds. These consonants are called in linguists 'Retroflex'.

"Saratchandra the next set; namely: त *ta* थ *tha* द *da* ध *dha* न *na* are linguistically labeled Dental consonants. These sounds are produced using the tongue to touch the back of the teeth. These sounds are softer, and used often in Hindi. Pay particular attention to this set. Notice we've been moving closer and closer to the lips with each set.

"The next set; namely: प *pa* फ *pha* ब *ba* भ *bha* म *ma* move us to the lips. If you say the English word 'boy' the 'b' is produced with the lips, and this is the same case with this set. These sounds are referred to in linguistics as Labial consonants, because they are produced with the lips.

"The next set of consonants; namely: य *ya* र *ra* ल *la* ळ *lla* व *va* are sometimes referred to as semi-vowels, because they are formed in the same part of the mouth as the vowels you learned in lesson one. They are formed with the tongue almost suspended in the mouth without touching any part of the inside of the mouth. These sounds are quite soft. य *ya* is pronounced like the 'y' in 'yellow.' र *ra* is pronounced like the 'r' in 'red.' ल *la* ळ *lla* are nearly pronounced the same; the difference being the ळ *lla* stretches the 'l' twice as long. The sound is slightly softer than the 'l' in 'letter'. व *va* is pronounced as a cross between the English 'w' and 'v' —almost like the 'r' in 'rubber' with a 'v' in front of it. The व *va* sound is different from the English 'v' in that the bottom lip doesn't touch the top teeth, like it does in English.

"The next set; namely: श *sha* ष *sha* स *sa* are known in linguistics as Silibants. In Hindi श *sha* is used often. ष *sha* on the other hand, not so much. ष *sha* is used in words from Sanskrit loanwords, only, actually. In Hindi both are pronounced the same, yet in Sanskrit the ष *sha* is distinguished as a 'retroflex' consonant; produced curling the tongue on the palate. Both, for your learning purposes, can be construed as the same, and pronounced like the English 'sh' as in 'Shhhh, be quiet!' स *sa* is pronounced like the English 's' as in 'sit.'

The next consonant ह *ha* is like the English 'h' in 'hotel' and is referred to in linguistics as an Aspirate, since it is a hard discharge of air. In Hindi and Sanskrit, ह *ha* also takes the form of a colon, i.e. ':' and occurs without a head stroke across the top of the syllable. This case usually comes at the end of a word, but can occur infrequently in the middle.

"The next set; namely: क्ष *ksha* त्र *tra* ज्ञ *jnya* श्र *shra* are conjunct consonants. They appear less frequently, but you should be familiar with them. Notice, however, how 'r' is looks like a back-slash, connected to another consonant, i.e. त्र *tra*.

"The last set; namely: ज़ za ड़ ra ढ़ rha फ़ fa are a special set of consonants, in that they are borrowed Persian words. They are not native Sanskrit words, and were borrowed during the middle ages. They are distinguished with a dot underneath them. ज़ za sounds like the English 'z' in 'zoo.' ड़ ra and ढ़ rha are a variation of ड ra ढ dha and फ़ fa sounds like the English 'f' as in 'farm'.

"Now take your time practicing these consonants. Learn them by associating them with the areas of your mouth your tongue touches or doesn't. It will be easier to learn them taking this approach.

"When I was learning Saratchandra I learned a set at a time. I practiced writing each letter, in each set, over and over again until I had that set memorized. Then, and only then, did I move onto the next set.

"Now I'll leave you be to practice. Incidentally, when you are practicing your writing, the part below the horizontal line should only hang about a third of the way between your notepad lines. Practice that part first, and then after you have written the stem, add the crossbar last. This is the way you write Devanagari.

"Here take these also. These are some flashcards to assist you with memorizing them. They are from indirectknowledge.com. They really helped me solidify memorizing them, once I had practiced the sets," taught Sita.

"Thank you Sita. I will begin practicing now," promised Saratchandra.

Sita and Saratchandra sat in Govinda's until the evening program began; after which, they left to go back to Sita's apartment. At Sita's, the two practiced their Hindi very intentionally until it was time for bed. The discipline that Sita exuded not only impressed Saratchandra, but it motivated him greatly to learn Hindi for himself in the same respect. He yearned for the day that he could converse with her fluently in Hindi.

Lesson 3

A few days passed, and Saratchandra had mastered the consonants. He learned that in Hindi, there is an inherent 'a' vowel, attached to the standalone consonants. Unlike the English 'k' the Devanagari 'क *ka*' possessed an 'a' when it was pronounced as a standalone consonant. This was a big a-ha he had.

Today, Saratchandra was off work, it was morning, and Sita and he had just finished their sadhana[10] at her apartment temple. Saratchandra had been staying at Sita's every day. They were becoming inseparable except when he went to work. It was great to have a devoutly religious friend, such as Sita. She had taught him a lot, and had taken him under her wing, so to speak.

Sita was an incredible cook. She, like Saratchandra, was a vegetarian. Most sattvika[11] Hindus are lacto-vegetarians. They do not eat meat, and hold the cow to be a sacred animal; namely, to be protected. The cow represents in the Hindu fold the essence of sattva qualities, given how the cow only gives milk freely, while never taking anything. It is a selfless animal, which Hindu's revere for its representation of selflessness; a quality highly valued in Hindu society.

"Sita, I have mastered lesson 2. Can I move on to lesson 3?" asked Saratchandra.

"As soon as you prove you've mastered both lesson 1 and 2," answered Sita.

"How shall I prove it?" inquired Saratchandra.

Sita didn't answer. Instead she reached in her backpack, and pulled out a test she had created for Saratchandra.

"Here," she insisted.

"What's this?" he asked.

"A test, to prove mastery," Sita responded.

"You want me to do it now?" asked Saratchandra.

"Yes. You have three minutes. Starting now," she said, handing him a pen.

Saratchandra looked at her as if she were crazy, and realizing she was serious, and time was ticking, frantically began the test. When he was finished, was immediately when she said, "Stop. Time up."

She took the test from him, and looked it over. Saratchandra was sweating the test, not knowing how well or not-so-well he did.

"100%. You pass!" said Sita.

"Awesome. Now can I start lesson 3?" he asked her.

"We can start, sure," said Sita, pulling out her notebook.

"Okay, so you've mastered the stand alone vowels and consonants. Now it is time to learn about conjunct characters. These are infused letters. In English, we have standalone letters, but in Hindi, many words possess letters which have been combined, to save space and time when writing the words.

"I introduced you to them in lesson 2. Remember the letters: क्ष *ksha* त्र *tra* ज्ञ *jnya* श्र *shra?*" she asked him.

"Yes. I remember, quite well," he answered.

"Well, in many Hindi words, the letters you've learned already, get shortened, and added to other letters. These will take time to learn, but you'll learn them easier when you start learning Hindi vocabulary words. At that time you'll see the consonants and vowels combined together so often, that you'll instinctively know them when you see them, and begin taking them for granted.

"Today, I want to teach you the vowel stems. The vowels you learned in lesson 1 are how the vowels appear in their standalone form, or when they appear at the beginning of a word.

"When vowels appear in the middle or at the end of a word, they take a shortened form. Again, this is to make writing concise as well as easier to comprehend the words at first glance.

"So today, I'll first teach you the vowel stems, and then introduce you to some of the more common conjunct consonants.

"After you master this lesson, Sarat, you will be ready to start learning some vocabulary, as well as be introduced to basic grammar. Then, once you learn grammar conventions and some vocabulary terms, I'll teach you sentences, which will allow you to learn some more complex sentences, verbs, at which time you can start communicating verbally in Hindi.

"It's a process though, so go at your own pace, and take your time learning. Until then, be patient, and keep learning. It doesn't matter how long it takes you, so long as you do not force learning, or 'try' to learn to rapidly. You'll actually learn faster if you take your time and do not get in a hurry. So go slow at first, so you can go fast. Okay?" said Sita.

"I'll take your advice. You have more experience than I do. I trust your wisdom," said Saratchandra.

Sita now shortened Saratchandra's name; calling him Sarat. This is common in Hindu culture. A two syllable name is easier to say, than a four syllable name. Saratchandra didn't mine whatsoever. Others at the temple, and at work, called him Sarat, too.

"Now for shortening vowels..." said Sita.

Shortened Vowel Stems

आ *aa* ा

इ *ĭ* ि

ई *ēē* ी

उ *uh* ु

ऊ *oo* ू

ए *ē* े

ऐ *aī* ै

ओ *ō* ो

औ *au* ौ

"Sarat, these are the vowel stems. Notice how there is not one for अ 'a'. This is because, as I have explained, each consonant has an inherent अ **a** sound already attached to it. If there is a vowel which follows the consonant, it simply takes the place of the already inherent अ **a**. Also in my list here, keep in mind that the dotted circles, next to each vowel stem is only a marker, and when writing should be omitted.

"Sarat, you should practice these vowel signs using an actual consonant, or more than one consonant, when practicing them. Doing so will help you see how they look, when connected to an actual letter. Here is an example to demonstrate, and get you started:

क ka + Vowel Signs

का kaa

कि kĭ

की kēē

कु kuh

कू koo

के kē

कै kai

को kō

कौ kau

"Now, I will demonstrate to you, some of the more common conjunct consonant forms," said Sita.

Common Conjunct Consonants

क् + क = क्क

क् + ख = क्ख

क् + ग = क्ग

च् + च = च्च

च् + छ = च्छ

न् + द = न्द

र् + म = र्म

प् + र = प्र

त् + र = त्र

ल् + ल = ल्ल

क् + त = क्त

न् + न = न्न

न् + द् + र = न्द्र

त् + त = त्त

"Sarat, practice these, yet understand there are many conjunctions not covered here, but which you will become exposed to as you learn more words in the future.

"Pay particular attention to 'r' as it can be written as: र when it is stand alone, or a backslash (e.g., क्र) or when preceding a consonant, such as the case with the word karma (e.g. कर्म) in which it becomes a curved sign on top of the cross bar.

"Also, Sarat, pay attention to nasalized letters; namely: न ण म ञ ङ as these are also written above the line as a dot, called a chandra-bindu (e.g., ॐ) when no other vowel is present. However, when a vowel, in the same word, extends above the hang-line, then the crescent beneath the dot is deleted; leaving only the dot to represent the nasalization (e.g., ◌). In the case of the latter, this sign is simply called a bindu; meaning, dot.

"So this is enough for you to practice for now.

Notes

[1] Dharma is the Sanskrit term for law or religion or duty. In this instance it means religious duty or obligation.

[2] Namakarana Samskara is a rite of passage, where one enters the Hindu fold, by receiving one's Hindu name. The name is given by a spiritual guru, i.e. teacher.

[3] Bhakti Yoga is the yoga of devotional service to the lord. Bhakti is a Sanskrit word for love or devotion.

[4] Rahasya Namah Sahasra literally means: Secret Names One Thousand, and is another name for the Shri Lalita Sahasranama.

[5] Devi means Goddess in Sanskrit.

[6] The Other Mind is what is referred to in this book at the unconscious or subconscious mind.

[7] The Mind is referring to the conscious mind or critical reasoning mind. This Mind is more limited, yet, ironically, more critical than the Other Mind.

[8] Bhajans are Hindu hymns sung in praise of Gods and Goddesses. Bhajans are Hindu devotional music.

[9] Aroti is the Hindu ritual of waving a ghee lamp in front of a murti.

[10] Sadhana is Sanskrit for spiritual practice.

[11] Sattvika is a Sanskrit term meaning 'of-pure-truth' and is attached to Sattva; the most rarefied guna in Samkya philosophy.

CHAPTER 4

Devotion, Obsession, or Control?

Surat was spending a lot of time with Sita. His life was transitioning away from his past, and to such a degree that a wakeup call was bound to happen.

"What do you mean?" Sarat's father asked, sounding upset.

"Dad, I've been staying with a girl," Sarat repeated.

"A girl? You live here. You have obligations here. Your Mitch and Michelle said they haven't seen you in a week! I think you need to re-evaluate your priorities son," said his dad.

"What do you mean?" asked Sarat.

"I mean you need to be here making sure that things get done. Mitch and Michelle will be graduating in May, but until then, I'm relying on you to take care of things.

"For crying-out-loud, I got a call from Mitch's teacher, and she said, 'He's not going to graduate, if he doesn't bring up his grades,' and Ryan or Sarat, or whatever your name is, I need you here helping out. You're a disappointment to me lately. I need you to step up and be responsible, and quit thinking about girls, and quit being selfish, and help me. Can you do that?" asked his father.

"Dad, I didn't know about Mitch's grades. I…"

"You didn't know about his failing marks, because you haven't been here. I put a roof over your head, and buy your food, and clothes, and all I ask from you in return is that you be here to help me out with the others. You just don't get it, do you?" interrupted his father.

"I get it. I'm sorry. I just…"

"Just be home, helping out. That's all I ask from you. I need you to be here. And, I'm concerned that you've been burying your head in all this religious fanaticism for far too long, and it's time to put a stop to it. You got me!?" his father conveyed very directly.

"Got you," said Sarat.

"Good. Now I have to leave out again tonight, and when I talk to Mitch and Michelle I want to hear that you've been around.

"Ryan, they rely on you, and so do I. We've always been a family, and, frankly, I'm concerned about you son," his father said to him.

"You're right dad. I haven't been very present lately. I'll start helping out more. I'm sorry," said Sarat.

"I'll hold you to it. Anyway, I have to make a few phone calls, and get packed. I'll won't be gone long, and then if you want to go off with girls, you can. Just, for now, help me out with the kids. Okay?" his dad asked.

"Okay."

Sarat had promised Sita he wouldn't be long. He was about to be a liar. This confrontation with his father came completely out of left-field. He wasn't expecting it at all. He was now sitting in his and Mitch's room, talking to Mitch about his poor performance in school.

Since his mother had abandoned the family when he was eleven, he had practically raised his Mitch and Michelle. His father had to struggle to work to make ends-meet. This meant being gone weeks at a time on the road.

Their dad made good money. Since Sarat was eleven, his father had never made less than $100,000 a year. It was the money that paid for their expensive home in Bowling Green, and the lush furnishings the family had always had. It paid for everything.

The problem was, the price tag attached to everything, which was, painfully, a father who wasn't a father, who was never around to handle anything. Not to mention the cost Sarat had to pay, which was taking on the responsibility of his younger siblings.

Sarat helped Mitch with his Physics homework, and talked him to a better state. Then saw his father off.

At ten-thirty Sarat was the only one up in the apartment. He was playing all this out in his mind. He was debating going over to Sita's so he wouldn't be perceived as a complete liar.

At eleven-twenty he was pulling up in front of her apartment. He was hoping she wouldn't mind being waken up, knowing she was usually in bed by ten o'clock.

"Sita, are you up?" asked Sarat, after knocking on her door.

There was no answer.

He knocked again, a little louder.

"Sita are you home?" he asked an octave up.

Still no answer.

Thinking it best not to wake her, he started back toward the direction of his car. Just as he approached, he heard her voice call out, "Sarat?"

He raced back to the apartment.

"Sita, sorry I didn't meet you at the temple, like planned. I got caught up with some family drama," he said to her. She was standing in the doorway, with the door partly opened.

"Come inside out of the cold," she said.

Once inside, she said, "It's late, tell me what's going on?"

"I got home. My father started in on my case about not being home to take care of my brother and sister. Anyway, he wants me to start being home to take care of them. I guess my brother Mitch isn't doing so well in school. Dad blames me.

"I'm so stressed out. I wanted to meet you, but to keep the peace, I had to wait until he left out again," said Sarat, hoping Sita would understand.

"I see," she said, looking aggravated at him.

"Yeah. So I will probably have to start staying over there more, at least until May, when Mitch and Michelle graduate.

"Anyway, I didn't want you to worry, or be upset, so I thought it best to come out here, and let you know what was going on. Sorry, I couldn't make it to temple this evening," he said to her.

"Are you staying here tonight?" she asked.
"Do you want me to?" he answered with a question.
"Do you want to?" she answered with another question.
"Of course, but..."
"Just go Sarat!" she interrupted.
"But..."
"Just go. Get out of my apartment," she demanded.
"Why are you being like this?" he asked, weirded out.
"Because I can," she said, "Now leave."

Sarat, was disappointed, shocked, and didn't know what else to do, except leave. So he left.

On the drive home, he replayed over and over the dialogue he had with Sita.

"What went wrong?" he thought.

"I don't know where I went wrong," he said to himself.

When he got back to the apartment he was exhausted by his emotions, and what he was feeling. He was not in a positive place mentally. Now resentment was setting in towards his brother, sister, and father. He was also feeling anxiety about his and Sita's relationship.

"Do we have a relationship?" he thought to himself.

"What am I going to do?" he wondered.

"What can I do?" he thought.

Sarat didn't sleep well that night. He got up early, to see his brother and sister off to school. He then took a shower and went to work.

At work he was distant from everyone in the warehouse.

"I don't want to be here anymore," he thought.

Most of the day was spent thinking about Sita and what transpired the night before.

After work, he went to the temple hoping she would be there. She wasn't.

He waited around until six-thirty, when the evening program started, and still no Sita.

He walked into the program, and began participating. He also wanted to pray about his situation.

A few minutes later, Sita appeared, but took a seat on the other side of the hall with some of the other female devotees. She didn't pay him any attention, and seemed to be more focused on the program, and worship.

This bugged him, and made him want her even more to notice him. He just wanted some type of resolution to whatever, was the problem. He still really didn't know what the problem was, or even if there was a problem. He sensed there was one though, by Sita's behavior the night before.

After the program, Sarat confronted Sita in Govinda's. She had gotten in line first, and was seated with some of the other female devotees, eating.

"Sita, can I speak to you?" Sarat asked her.

She just looked at him, expectantly.

When he didn't say anything, she ignored him, and went back to eating. Her face was expressionless.

"Sita, can I speak to you in private?" Sarat asked her.

"Excuse me," Sita said, speaking to the other devotees she had been in discourse with.

Sita stood up and walked to the other side of the room. Sarat followed her like a sheep.

"What's up?" she asked him.

"I don't know. What is up? You're upset with me and I have no idea why? Can you please tell me what's wrong? What did I do to offend you?" Sarat asked Sita.

"Sarat…

"Sarat, I think you should focus on your family; not on me.

"Sarat, I think it's what's best for both of us.

"I think that's what's best," she said to him.

"Okay. But, I still don't understand. I still sense that you're upset with me.

"I want to be with you Sita. I care about you," he said.

"I have to go," she said, turning to walk away.

Sarat let her go, without another word. He felt like he should have been more persistent, but another part felt like he didn't have anything left to say. It was frustrating. Sad really, watching the girl leave, unable to make her stay. What's a young man to do?

Sarat reentered the temple, and proceeded back down to Govinda's where he sat in silence and finished eating. In his silence, he wasn't praying, but rather feeling rejected, and dejected. His depression and sadness were growing by the minute.

Feeling are funny that way. You can be in one state of mind, happy and thrilled with your life, and in another instance be feeling your lowest. You can go from happy to sad to deeply depressed in the span of 24 hours. That's what happened to Sarat.

Sarat got up, dumped his paper plate in the trashcan, and sadly left the temple. Once outside he walked around the front, towards the alley, where his car was parked. When he got into his car he broke down crying. He was crying and crying and sobbing his eyes out like there was no tomorrow. It was the most emotional he had been since his brother's funeral –and, that was a long time ago.

Another devotee girl had parked next to him. Sarat had noticed her walking toward his car, and was trying to duck down, so as to not be noticed. It was too late. The girl had already recognized him.

Prema, was another American Hindu girl, who had grown up in the Hindi faith. Her parents had met during the late 70s and become interested in a religion that advocated peace and tolerance, and, after finding Hinduism, decided to convert. Prema had never known the reality of any other faith—she was Hindu.

Prema had found Sarat attractive though never approached him, or shown an interest, because he was always around Sita. She just assumed they were together, since they were always together these days.

It must have been something in the cold winter air, because this night, this very intense night, Prema decided to introduce herself to Sarat. This was completely out of character for her, but something just told her to do it.

"Are you alright," Prema asked, knocking on the driver side window.

"I'm fine," replied Sarat, trying to sound masculine and strong.

"You don't sound fine," said Prema.

Sarat just waited for a moment, hoping she would leave him alone. She didn't.

"What's the matter?" Prema asked him.

"Why does anything have to be the matter?" he asked her back.

"Something's got to be bothering you. You are sitting in a cold car, crying, and this tells me that there's something the matter. So what's the matter? Maybe I can help," she suggested to him.

Sarat sat up in his seat, and looked out the window for a brazen second at her, and noticed she was holding her arms, freezing to death, shivering. He rolled down his window, and said, "You can get in. I don't bite."

Prema, smiled at him, and walked around to the passenger side, and got into Sarat's car.

"I'm Prema," she said.

"I'm Sur..."

"Sarat," she finished his sentence.

"Right," he said.

"I know who you are. I was at your namakarana samskara.

"Anyway, what is troubling you? I saw you crying, and something just told me I should talk to you," she said.

"To be perfectly honest, I'm not sure what's bothering me, really.

"You know that girl Sita?" he asked Prema.

"Your girlfriend," she said, wanting to find out if they were in face boyfriend and girlfriend.

"She's not my girlfriend. She's just a friend. Actually, I'm not sure what she is. She's been acting weird the last couple days. I cannot figure her out," he confessed.

"Well, what's she doing, that leads you to believe this?"

"I was staying with her, but then my dad, who is a truck driver..."

Sarat finished recounting the entire situation to Prema. She sat there listening, only occasionally asking a question, to gain clarity, when she was confused.

After Sarat was finished, Prema said to him, "Maybe the advice she gave you is good advice. I don't think it really matters what her reasoning is. I think you should just respect it, and move on.

"Sita is a headstrong girl, not really girlfriend material I don't think.

"You have a job, a good family, and are a spiritual person, and you'll meet the right girl, I feel," said Prema.

"I don't know. Maybe you're right. Perhaps I do need to back away from her, and move on, and focus on what's important with my family," reasoned Sarat.

"Don't worry about it. Just pray about it. God will show you happiness again Sarat," said Prema.

"Thanks!" he said to her.

"You are really welcome Sarat," said Prema, starry-eyed, and infatuated with Sarat.

"Well, I guess I better get home. Thanks for being a friend," said Sarat, feeling better.

"That's what friends are for.

"Are you coming to temple tomorrow?" she asked him.

"Yes. I will be here tomorrow at six-thirty. Are you coming?" he asked her back.

"Yes.

"If you want we can sit together," she suggested to him.

"That sounds nice. I'll see you tomorrow," Sarat said.

"See you tomorrow," she said, smiling like a young girl in love with a boy, opening the car door to get out.

The next day, Sarat went to work, helped his brother with his school work, and went to the temple. When he arrived Prema was wearing a beautiful red and white sari. She had her hair spectacularly done, and flowers arranged in such a unique manner that it set her apart from the other girls.

Prema had soft skin, a round face, and a pale complexion, but was less pale than Sita. She had color in her cheeks, and youth in her voice and mannerisms. She was eighteen, but looked like she was a child. She was short, and youthful.

When Sarat arrived, and saw her, he nearly did a double take. She was much more beautiful than he recalled from the night before. His eyes definitely couldn't stop staring at her.

When he walked toward her, she said, "It looks like today is a better day for you."

"Yes. Much better. I'm sorry about last night. I didn't mean to cry on your shoulder about all my drama," he stated, smiling at her charmingly.

"Don't be silly; that's what friends are for Sarat," said Prema.

Prema walked into the temple hall with Sarat, and brought him over to where she usually sat. Prema had a couple girlfriends, and they were all giggles, smiling at the two.

A few minutes later Sita walked in, and made her way over to a different spot. At first she didn't notice Sarat, sitting with Prema. When she did notice, Sarat noticed her noticing. When she notice this she closed her eyes, raised her hands in prayer pose, and said a prayer.

During the worship, Sita was completely engaged, but Sarat was not, and he couldn't stop thinking about how weird it felt not sitting next to Sita. Prema was good eye-candy, and a sweet girl, but he didn't know her as well as he did Sita.

"Sarat, I'll be right back, I have to go to the restroom. I'll try not to be very long, okay?" asked Prema.

"Sure. I'll be here waiting for you," Sarat answered.

Prema arose and gracefully, walked toward the restroom. She looked at Sita, and smiled at her. Sita, acted not to notice. She noticed.

A short time later, Prema came back and started again at Sita, and then made her way back to Sarat, who was oblivious of what was going on between the two girls.

"Honey, I'm back. Sorry it took me so long," she said, slipping her arm around his.

In his mind he was thinking all sorts of thought. Outwardly though he remained calm.

Sarat thought to himself, "She's calling me honey, holding my arm, and being apologetic when she shouldn't. What's going on? Does she think we're together? Her friends are acting strangely giddy, and keep looking at us sitting together. How embarrassing. I bet Sita is upset. What am I doing? This was a mistake, I think. Too late now though. What am I going to do? I'm treading on thin ice, and it's cracking all around me." He thought all those thoughts and more. Interesting what the mind comes up with when you're in unchartered waters, isn't it?

After the worship, Prema walked on his side to Govinda's, and said, "Take a seat Sarat, I will serve you food," and proceeded to get plates for both of them.

Sarat just complied. It was pointless, he reasoned, to argue with her.

Sita was sitting a few tables down, engaged in her Hindi lessons. Sarat, desperately wanted to talk to her, but knew better. Out of the side of her eye, Sita observed Prema serving Sarat. Prema's girlfriends eventually made their way to their table and took seats. Prema and the girls talked, and had a good time, and Sarat pretended to be having a good time also, but he couldn't take his mind off Sita.

"Sarat ji, can I get you more to eat? You must still be hungry. Let me get you something more," said Prema.

"No. I'm full, I'm good," said Sarat.

"Well, let me take your empty plate and discard it, then," she said, standing up, taking Sarat's plate.

"Thanks Prema," he said.

Prema didn't say a word. Not saying a word, was more of a statement than anything she could have said. Sita, Prema's girlfriends, and other devotees sitting nearby all noticed this act of devotion. A lot of thoughts were thought in that room. Many people were wondering what happened between Sarat and Sita, and why was he sitting with Prema, and what was the nature of their relationship. It looked like, by others, that Prema and Sarat were an item.

"Sarat ji, I have a favor to ask of you," said Prema looking at him fondly.

"Sure, what do you need?" he asked. He felt indebted by all the attention she was giving to him.

"I wasn't able to drive here tonight. Can you give me a ride home tonight?" she inquired.

There was a hesitant pause. It was recognizable by anyone paying attention.

"Certainly, Prema, I can give you a ride home," said Sarat. He didn't want to, but, again, he felt indebted by her kindness.

Sita heard this conversation. She was fed up listening, and so gathered her things and left to go back to her own apartment. Sitting in her car, she thought, "Why are guys so dumb."

A short while later, Prema asked Sarat, "Honey are you ready?" and he replied, "Sure," agreeably.

When they walked out to Sarat's car, she waited for him to open the car door for her. When he did, she smiled at him sweetly.

"So, where to?" asked Sarat.

Just then Prema's cell phone rang, and it was her mom on the phone.

"Hi mom!" said Prema.

"Prema, are you still staying with your friend Beka?" asked her mom.

"Yes mom," Prema answered. Sarat couldn't hear the conversation, and so was oblivious of what was being discussed.

When the conversation was over, Prema put on a look of upset. And looked trouble.

"Is everything okay?" asked Sarat.

"Not really," said Prema.

"Why? What's wrong?" he inquired.

"My mom and dad are out of town, and the house is locked, because they thought I was staying with my friend Beka. But the problem is Beka's mom is away on business, and Beka's dad won't let me stay there, and I don't have a key to get in. I don't have anywhere to go," said Prema, pretending to cry and be upset.

"So where should I take you?" Sarat asked her, concerned.

"I don't know Sarat," said Prema.

Sarat was baffled. He thought to himself, "Unbelievable!" He wanted to off-load Prema, who had been acting like they were a couple all night long. He was too nice to be mean, but a part of him wanted to bolt, and leave the whole situation. Now he couldn't. He had a Prema on his hands—a Prema he couldn't get rid of!

Prema just sat there in his car, in the parking lot, waiting for Sarat to come up with what to say next. After a couple minutes, trying his best to come up with something, out of ideas, he said, "Prema, do you think your parents would object to you staying the night at my house? You could sleep in my sister's room, if you like," he suggested to her.

"Are you sure?" she asked.

"I mean, I don't care, if your parents are alright with it. Can you call them?" he asked her.

"It's okay with them. I'm an adult, and they trust me," she responded.

Sarat had forgotten she was of age, because of how young she appeared and acted.

Sarat started the car, and began pulling out of the parking lot. As he was driving, Prema was complimenting him, and talking his head off.

When Sarat pulled into the driveway, she sat in the car until he walked around to the passenger side, opened her door, and helped her out.

When she stepped into the apartment, Mitch was sitting in the front room, eating a plate of something, and Michelle was sitting on the floor in one corner, finishing her homework for chemistry.

"Mitch, Michelle, this is Prema. She's homeless tonight, so I invited her to stay with us tonight. Michelle is it alright if Prema sleeps with you in your room?" asked Sarat.

"Sure, I don't mind. Hi, Prema," greeted Michelle.

"Hi, Prema," also greeted Mitch.

Both Mitch and Michelle assumed that Prema was the same girl Sarat had been seeing for all those past weeks. They didn't keep up with their brother's love life. Neither of them really cared one way or the other. They were both preoccupied with their own pastimes.

"Sarat, can you show me the deck outside? I want to look around, if it's okay with you?" asked Prema.

Sarat agreeably said, "Sure. It's right this way," and proceeded to show her the deck.

On the deck, Prema said, "Sarat, can you hold me, I'm freezing?"

Sarat was feeling a little nervous about holding her, but didn't want to make her feel uncomfortable, so just accepted her in his arms. Prema held him tightly, so he would reciprocate, and like a charm it worked miracles.

Then, looking up at him, and him looking down at her, she smiled at him, closed her eyes, and puckered her lips, separating them slightly, leaving her mouth slightly opened to accept Sarat's kiss.

Sarat's heart started beating faster and faster. He was nervous, parts of his body stiffened, and without thinking, acting purely on animal instincts, he kissed Prema on the forehead, like one kisses a daughter or a young niece, and put his chin on top of her head. He couldn't do it. He couldn't make her his first French kiss.

In the nick-of-time, Michelle, opened the sliding glass door, and asked, "Sarat, Mitch wants to know if you will help him with some of his homework problems?"

"Tell him I'll be right there," said Sarat.

Michelle walked back in, shutting the door behind her.

"My sister was coming," Sarat stated; meant to imply why he didn't kiss her.

"Oh. Good thinking," said Prema.

"I guess I better get in here and help Mitch. Michelle is probably ready to tuck-in for the night, so you'll probably want to hand out with her in her bedroom a bit, so she can explain things. You know what I mean," said Sarat to Prema.

"Okay. That sounds like a plan," said Prema, mildly upset that she didn't get her kiss; but happy none-the-less that she was embraced, and had a new boyfriend.

Once inside, Sarat sat over beside Mitch, and Prema joined Michelle in her room to figure out her sleeping arrangements.

"Are you going to marry my brother?" Michelle asked Prema.

"I hope so," said Prema.

"My brother must care a lot about you," commented Michelle.

"Yeah, you think so?" asked Prema.

"Yeah, he's never had a girlfriend before," confessed Michelle.

"Do you think he loves me?" asked Prema.

"He must," said Michelle.

"I love your brother," Prema confided.

"You sure are pretty! And sweet! My brother is lucky to have you in his life. I cannot wait for you two to marry," shared Michelle.

Prema woke up at three o'clock in the morning, and nudged Michelle awake.

"Wake-up sleepy head," Prema said to Michelle.

I don't know if Michelle, had ever awoken that early, ever, in her entire life. She was out of it, fighting to wake-up.

"I'm up! But, why am I up?" she asked Michelle.

"It is time to go to Temple," said Prema.

"Time to go to temple?" asked Michelle, out of it.

"Yes. You need to wake your brothers up, so we can get there on time," said Prema, quite serious, but kindly.

"I don't think they want to go," reasoned Michelle.

"Want to go or not, we're going," pushed Michelle.

Michelle, wasn't about to argue with this girl she barely knew. She complied, and got up and put on some pajamas and a tank top and walked to the boy's room.

"Mitch, Ryan, wake up!" Michelle said, knocking on their door loudly.

Soon Sarat poked his head out and said, "What's going on?"

"You need to talk to this girl. Now!" said Michelle.

"Okay. Give me a minute. I'll be right there," the half-awake Sarat answered.

A few minutes later, once dressed, Sarat entered Michelle's room. Prema was making her and Michelle's bed, and straightening up the room.

"Michelle is in the shower, we'll be ready soon. Are you and Mitch going to bathe first?" Prema asked.

"What do you mean?" Sarat asked her.

"Are you going to bathe, before temple?" Prema asked him again.

"Temple?" Sarat asked, with an upward inflexion, denoting a question.

"Sarat, get Mitch up. You two get a shower. Michelle and I will be ready by the time you two are," she instructed.

"Michelle and Mitch are not Hindu. I thought today we could skip, and just catch up at the evening program," suggested Sarat.

"Sarat, Michelle and I want to go. It will be good for you to go, and so better then that Mitch come along as well, so he won't have to be by himself. Besides I can grill him on his homework. It is what your father wanted, remember," she framed.

Sarat wanted to argue, but knew it would be a waste of time. He was beginning to think that Prema had some type of mental disorder. This week, he reasoned, was turning out to be a lost cause.

To seem agreeable, Sarat said, "You're right, I'll get Mitch up and going. We'll be ready soon."

"Alright, love you. See you soon," she said.

"Alright, love you," he repeated in his head, as he shut the door and walked back to Mitch's and his room.

"Now she loves me?" Sarat said to himself, unable to get the thought out of his mind.

"Mitch get up," commanded Sarat.

"What the..." responded Mitch, confused.

"Get up. Just get up. It's Prema, she is insisting we go to the temple this morning," relayed Sarat.

"Man, you're crazy if you think I'm getting up this early. I definitely not going to some Hindu temple with you and your girlfriend."

He added, "You're crazy if you think that's happening," and put his pillow over his head, to block out the light.

"Listen, Mitch, I know. I know. Seriously, though, just this once. I'll never ask you to do this again."

"Please I have to get her back to the temple, and get rid of her. I need your help to make that happen," said Sarat.

"Bro, she's your problem. Not mine. I'm out of it," argued Mitch.

Sarat let him be. He took a shower and got himself dressed in a dhoti, and met Prema and Michelle out in the front room a short while later.

"Where's Mitch?" demanded Prema.

"He doesn't want to come. He's sleeping," Sarat said.

Prema bypassed arguing about it. She without hesitation walked toward Mitch's and Sarat's room and opened the door.

"You need to get up!" demanded Prema.

Mitch, having no shirt on, turned around, and said, "I'm not going. Please you all leave me alone. I'm tired of all this craziness."

"Mitch this is the reason you're failing school. You have not motivation, and no guidance, and you think you know what's best for you—now get up! You buster are going to be a part of this family, whether you like it or not," said Prema, taking his pillow off his bed.

"You're crazy. Bat shit crazy," said Mitch.

Prema stormed out of the room crying. They were fake tears, but real enough.

"He cussed me Sarat. Are you going to let him get away with that?" demanded Prema, carrying on.

"Look I don't want any problems. Maybe we should just let him stay and rest," suggested Sarat to her.

"You need to step up and be the adult Sarat. The family that prays together; stays together."

"I can't believe you are being weak, giving in to your brother's rebellion. You need to be the adult, and take control," said Prema.

"Prema, I'm with Sarat, I think maybe we should just leave Mitch here," said Michelle, taking Sarat's side.

Mitch could hear everything. Prema had left his bedroom door open. He was fully awake now. Pissed, but fully awake.

"Sarat, get your brother," demanded Prema, like a spoilt little girl, used to getting her own way.

"Huh!" sighed Sarat.

"I'll talk to him," said Sarat, walking toward their room.

Sarat sat on Mitch's bed, and said, "Listen buddy, I don't ask much from you..."

But before he could plead another word, Mitch got out of bed, grabbed some clothes, and said, "I just want you to know I can't stand that girl. I'm doing this just to help you out, but don't ever ask me to do this shit again," and stomped his was to the shower, angry.

Sarat walked back to the front room and said, "Okay. Mitch is getting a shower. He'll be ready soon."

Prema just smiled, and said, "Show him how to put on a dhoti and a kurta."

Sarat just sighed and closed his eyes and walked back to the bedroom.

When he was gone out of sight Prema asked Michelle, "Can I stay here this week with you guys? My parents are going out of town, and I don't have a place to stay."

Michelle was lost for words to say and to be agreeable said, "Sure. I guess."

Michelle wanted to say no, but didn't want to stir up another confrontation with Prema.

"I think I'm going to like having you as a sister," said Prema.

"Me too," said Michelle agreeably.

A short while later out came Sarat and Mitch dressed in dhoti and kurta's.

"You two look very handsome," said Prema smiling.

"Mitch quit slouching, and stand up taller. You're a man, you need to act like one," said Prema.

Mitch didn't want to argue anymore. He knew Prema was just trying to start crap with him. He stood taller, intentionally, and asked Prema, "Like this?"

She said, "Yes. Now you look very powerful and manly! Very good."

On the way to the temple, Mitch remained quiet, as did Sarat. Prema and Michelle talked like they had known each other all their life. Michelle was starting to really admire Prema's ability to manipulate everyone into doing what she wanted. She also like having her as an ally, and it was nice having a new female friend to share things with.

Sarat pulled into the parking lot in the alley behind the temple. It was nearly four o'clock, and some of the other devotees were arriving and walking into the temple.

Mitch stayed close to Sarat, feeling weirded out by the strange environment, wishing in his head that he had not agreed to come.

Michelle stayed close to Prema, while she explained some things to her about the temple, and Hinduism.

Inside, Prema took Michelle to where three of her other friends were sitting, and introduced her. The other girls were very friendly and courteous to her. Michelle was actually having a good time meeting the new girls; enjoying herself, glad she had decided to come.

"Mitch?" yelled Prema from across the hall.

"Yeah?" he replied.

"Come over here, I want to introduce you to some people," said Prema.

Mitch looked at Sarat. Sarat was reading his mind, knowing he was wanting to be anywhere but there. But kept quiet.

Mitch gave a look to Sarat of his upset, and then looked at Prema and said, "I'm coming."

Prema was controlling everything. She was very manipulative.

Mitch walked over to where Michelle and Prema were sitting, and Prema introduced Mitch to her three girlfriends.

"Mitch this is Radha, this is Siya, and this is Adhita. Girls this is Mitch. He's Sarat's brother," she introduced.

"Hi. Nice to meet you all," said Mitch politely.

Prema kept beautiful company. All three of her friends were highly attractive, and divine looking. They were very pretty girls. Mitch was captivated, and in fact, felt a little shy around them.

"Adhita, can you take Mitch and show him around the temple, before the morning program starts?" Prema asked her friend.

Ahita humble stood up and said to Mitch, "Come I'll show you around," and insinuated like she expected him to follow her. In her head, she was crushing hard on Mitch. He was very cute, and dhoti clad, she assumed he was a devout Hindu.

Mitch followed her.

"That's a pretty name Ahita," remarked Mitch to her.

"It means in Sanskrit 'Scholar,'" revealed Ahita.

Mitch was thinking to himself how ironic it was that he was walking around with a girl named Scholar, when it was him who was failing his senior year of high school. Ah the lessons of life.

When Ahita had showed Mitch Govinda's and explained how they would be eating after the program, she asked him, "How come I haven't seen you here before? I didn't even know Sarat had a brother."

Mitch said, "I'm still in high school, and just haven't been before."

"How do you like the temple?" she asked him.

"It is very beautiful!" he remarked.

"Very peaceful, isn't it?" she asked.

"Very peaceful," he agreed.

Mitch was having a better time. He had met a pretty girl, and actually was grateful for being introduced to Ahita. But he'd never admit that to Prema. He still wasn't sure about her. He was however feeling regretful of the harsh words he threw at her earlier.

When Ahita took Mitch back to the temple room, she introduced him to her parents, who were likewise very kind people. When they found out that he was Sarat's brother, they were even happier to know him. They knew Sarat was a nice boy, and assumed the same about his brother. It's interesting, the psychology of association, don't you think?

When Sita arrived, she noticed new people at the temple. Sarat tried to make his way over to her to tell her his brother and sister were there, but Prema kept that from happening.

Sensing his intention to talk to Sita, she rushed to him, and urged him strongly to come and join her and his family.

Sarat complied and joined her to sit with his brother and sister. The group of friends were all having a good time. Mitch was even laughing at Ahita's jokes and Sarat could tell, as well as Michelle, that Mitch was infatuated with Ahita.

After the program, Sita slipped out, and Prema was in the restroom, so Sarat took the opportunity to slip out too, to try and talk to her.

"Sita?" said Sarat.

Sita stopped in her tracks and debated turning around. She had paused for too long, so knew she better turn around. She didn't want to though.

"Yeah?" said Sita.

"My brother and sister are here," said Sarat.

"That's awesome," said Sita, truly happy for him.

"Yeah...It's a long story, but Prema instigated it. I'd love to tell you the story sometime.

"Are you not staying for prasadam?" asked Sarat to her.

"I can't, I have to get back to the house," said Sita.

"Oh. I see. Anyway, I've missed our Hindi lessons," he said.

"If you are committed to learning Hindi, you can come to my apartment after your work, and I will teach you lessons. That is if you don't think that Prema will get upset with you," said Sita.

Girls could be fierce. They always have a way of making a direct point to boys. Usually, saying things boys don't want to hear.

"I am my own man. I can do what I want. I'll come today straight after work," said Sarat confidently.

"Okay. Well...I guess I'll see you then," said Sita, without any excitement in her voice.

In Sita's mind she was happy that Sarat wanted to come and study Hindi. She was still mad at him. She was even jealous of Prema. She would never admit this to Sarat though.

"Okay. See you then," said Sarat.

As Sarat made his way back into Govinda's Mitch and Michelle were sitting with Prema's friends. Mitch was sitting right next to Ahita. Prema must have still been in the restroom.

"He guys, have any of you seen Prema?" asked Sarat?

"She's in the restroom, Sarat. She'll be here soon," said Siya.

"Okay," said Sarat, taking a seat at the table.

It was nearly time for the Prasad line to open. Prema had returned.

"Michelle, come with me and the girls," said Prema.

"Why, where are we going?" asked Michelle.

"Prasad line," said Prema.

"Oh. Okay," said Michelle, confused.

At the Prasad line, Prema instructed Ahita to prepare a plate for Mitch. Michelle was educated about Indian vegetarian cuisine, and helped to select food for her to eat, which she might like. Prema also taught her the significance of where to put the vegetable on the plate, where to put the rice and dhal, and roti. All of this was new to Michelle. In her mind though, she thought the food looked tasty.

Back at the table the girls sat, while Prema and Ahita stayed stood. Prema served Sarat, and Ahita served Mitch. Mitch was in awe of this luxurious attention by Ahita, while Sarat had come to accept it as custom.

"Mitch, let me get you some more when you require," said Ahita.

"Thank you Ahita," he said, smiling. She smiled back at him.

After eating, Sarat explained to Prema how he had to get Mitch and Prema back in time for school, and how he himself needed to get to work.

Michelle overhearing this said, "Ryan. Sorry, I mean Sarat. I invited Prema to stay with us for a week, since her parents are out of town for a week."

"You did?" asked Sarat, feeling uneasy.

"If there's no problem!" said Prema.

"Umm... Yeah, umm..., No problem," he answered.

Sarat had a problem. He couldn't get rid of Prema. Things were getting out of hand. He liked her, didn't love her, and sometimes wish he'd never met her. He was grateful for her friendship, but things were being pushed on him by her, and she was very slippery and manipulative. He didn't know her intentions, but they made him feel uneasy, yet sometimes he really got pleasure from her pushiness; like this morning with how she handled Mitch. A lot was going on in Sarat's mind.

Prema was playing her cards well. She knew how to get what she wanted. She was an expert at it. She always got her way. Even with her parents and friends.

"Sarat, please can we stop at the Indian grocery, on the way back to the apartment. I need some groceries, and I want to get Michelle a sari for tomorrow, okay?" asked Prema, humbly; like she was the perfect Hindu wife.

"Sure," said Sarat.

"Michelle, we'll pick a pretty sari for you. This place is very perfect for buying saris. You'll see," said Prema.

"Awesome," said Michelle.

In the Indian grocery store, Michelle and Prema walked to the clothing section, and found a beautiful white and green paisley sari for Michelle. Prema then took Michelle down the aisles and explained to her about Indian vegetarian cooking, and what certain ingredients tasted like. Michelle was impressed with Prema's knowledge and happy for the attention, she was showing her.

After she was done shopping, she found Mitch and Sarat, and asked if she should pay for the items.

"No. I'll pay," said Sarat.

Prema smiled at him, and he smiled back at her. Something about Prema was fascinating and exciting and her mannerisms and the way she carried herself was unlike any girl he'd ever met. Mitch was even beginning to start liking Prema. He, like his brother, was captivated by her; almost hypnotized by her ways.

"Mitch, when we get to the house, you'll take in the groceries, and Sarat, you'll get ready for work, and Michelle I'll show you where the groceries should go. I'll teach you how to cook tonight. It'll be so much fun, you'll see. Mitch after you bring in the groceries, you should dress for school, and then all of can go together. That sounds like a good plan, doesn't it Sarat?" asked Prema.

"Sounds good to me. You have it all figured out Prema. You seem to always have things figured out," he said, smiling at her.

Prema just smiled, saying not a word. She was happy. She was something else.

Everyone did as they were instructed, and complied with the way Prema wanted things. On the way driving to the high school, Prema quizzed Mitch on his problems. She was mean, when he didn't get an answer correct. He hated her confrontation, because it was worse than his own. He had finally met his match, and met someone more argumentative than himself.

At school Mitch took his test and scored an A+ getting every question right, along with the bonus questions. He wouldn't have scored so high had it not been for Prema's grilling him and scolding him. After he got his grade he hated loving her so much.

Sarat went to work, and was in a happy mood. He was happy the morning had ended on a positive note, but concerned about his girl problems, and what the outcome of all this Sita and Prema stuff would be. There couldn't be a positive outcome, he concluded in his mind.

At four o'clock the warehouse was slow, and so Sarat cut out and headed to Sita's for his Hindi lesson, and to share with her all that happened.

"Sita, its Sarat," said Sarat, after knocking on her door.

"Namaste Sarat, come inside," said Sita.

"Can we talk?" asked Sarat.

"Come and sit," she invited.

Sarat made himself at home, as he always felt like he was at home at Sita's.

"Sita, I want to explain about Prema," said Sarat.

"Explain," she commanded.

An hour later, Sarat had thrown everything out on the table, and shared every honest detail with Sita.

"Sita, I tell you all this, because I love you. I'm in love with you. I want to be with you. I do not love Prema. I love you only!" confessed Sarat.

Sita smiled when she heard this, and saying nothing, began crying.

"Girls are so emotional," thought Sarat, watching her.

"Sarat, I don't know what to say except pray. I love you to. God may have other plans for us though. I know my dharma, and where my place is.

"I don't want to see you hurt. I don't want to be hurt. Nobody wants to be hurt. Not even Prema. Nobody.

"I will teach you Hindi. We'll leave the rest to God. You must choose your choices well. They are your choices. I will not be mad at you either way things go. I will only be happy for you. That is what you do when you love someone.

"Now shall I quiz you on your previous lessons to see if you are ready to move on to lesson 4?" said Sita.

"I'm ready," said Sarat.

Sita took out her notebook, from her backpack, and pulled out a quiz which already had Sarat's name on it.

"Take this. You have five minutes only," stated Sita.

Sarat didn't wait even a second, as he had with Sita's last test. He knew she was serious about these tests.

"Finished," he said.

"You have two more minutes. Do you want to take those minutes to look over your answers, to make sure you got them right?" she asked.

"No need. They are all right," said Sarat, confident they were all right.

Sarat had been practicing religiously, in the hopes that he would mend his relationship with Sita, and she might begin teaching him Hindi again.

Sita took the test, and reviewed his answers, and found none wrong. She didn't compliment him. She didn't want to inflate his ego any more than Prema had been doing.

"Sarat, now I will teach you lesson four," said Sita, taking out her notebook.

"In this lesson we will explore some everyday conversation, some grammar mechanics, and some vocabulary terms.

"I will teach you grammar first, then give you the vocabulary terms to memorize, then some sentences to study and to help solidify your learning and give you context to understand how to apply the lesson. Everything will be done in Hindi Devanagari script, and not in Roman script; except, for the English explanations of the lesson. These will be taught in English for your understanding.

"Each lesson I give you, Sarat, you must master before going on to the next. Each lesson will build on the next. Understand?" she asked Sarat.

"Yes. I clearly understand Sita," said Sarat, happy he was there spending time with her. He was happy she admitted loving him. It sealed in his mind that he wanted her and only her. He still had a problem though, but it would take a force higher than himself to help him with that problem.

Lesson 4

"Sarat, In Hind, it is best to learn the personal pronouns first. Personal pronouns are probably what you learned way back in third grade; namely, I, you, he, she, it, them, and they.

"In Hindi there are singular and plural pronouns. I'll write them for you:

Singular	Plural
I मैं	We हम

You	तू	You	तुम, आप
He, She, It	यह, वह	They	ये, वे

"Sarat, in English there is a single pronoun 'you' for both singular and plural. In Hindi there is a distinction. The pronoun तू is singular, and references children or someone on an intimate encounter. The pronoun तुम is used to reference someone casually, or someone in a lesser role than yourself. Even though it is listed as plural, it can be used in singular contexts as well. The pronoun आप is used to refer to people of a higher class, or people whom represent strangers, or people whom deserve respect (e.g., older people, parents, grandparents, bosses, etc.). आप is used most commonly in speaking to others. When in doubt always use आप. It can also be used in both referring to one person or more than one person.

"Sarat, in English there is a distinction between masculine and feminine pronouns. For example, she and he. In Hindi, it is proximity to the speaker that is recognized when referencing someone. For example, यह and ये reference someone or something nearby; whereas वह and वे reference something further away. Some people like to think of यह, वह respectively as this and that. Same thing with ये, वे as being respectively these and those. I think it is a good idea to think of them like this, because something that is close by we call 'this' and something further away we call 'that'. In the plural sense it would be, 'these' and 'those'. Make sense?" asked Sita.

"Very good sense. Thanks!" answered Sarat.

"One last point, and we'll move on. The pronouns यह, वह do not sound as they look. They are actually pronounced conversationally the same as their plural complements ये, वे. This is one of those rare instances of a Hindi word, not corresponding with how it should sound. Just keep it in mind.

"Okay, great. Now for the verb 'to-be' which in Hindi called होना which relates in everyday conversations to the pronouns. In English, it looks something like this:

I am	You are
He is	They are
It is	We are

"You get the idea. These are all in the present tense. In other words, 'I am here now.' Or, 'You are here now.' The present tense is what we'll focus on now.

"In Hindi there are corresponding present tense verbs which reference these pronouns, too. Let's see them.

SINGULAR		PLURAL	
I	मैं हूँ	We	हम हैं
YOU	तू है	You	तुम हो, आप हैं
HE, SHE, IT	यह है, वह है	They	ये हैं, वे हैं

"Notice how adding the present tense verb differentiate with regard to singular and plural, based on nasalization. The dot added to the singular form, makes it indicative of referring to more than one person, place or thing.

"Sarat ji, in Hindi, we call this changing of a verb, conjugation. What I have just showed you is how to conjugate the most common verb 'to-be', i.e. होना into the present tense for each pronoun. As in English these verb tenses will change, but we'll get to those changes as we move through these lessons.

"Now I want to teach you another difference between English and Hindi; namely, word order.

"In an English sentence, we say, 'I am Sita,' which is first the subject, then verb, and then the object. In Hindi the word order changes to subject, object, and then verb. In my opinion it is nice having the verb tagged on the end of a sentence. That's my personal opinion.

"So the same sentence would read, 'I Sita am.' In Hindi this simple present tense sentence would read, मैं सीता हूं।

Notice at the end of a Hindi sentence, in place of a period, I used a vertical bar?" asked Sita.

"Yeah, I notice that," confirmed Sarat.

"Yes, in Hindi imperative sentences and declarative sentences use the vertical bar to end with. Interrogative sentences use a question mark. Exclamatory sentences use an exclamation mark. So think if it ends in a period, it now ends in a vertical bar. The rest stays the same. Commas are used just like in English sentences. Pretty easy, eh?" asked Sita.

"Very easy!" exclaimed Sarat.

"I think this is really basic stuff for you, and being so bright Sarat, I think it is okay to take you a little further. I'll therefore end this lesson by teaching you some intransitive verbs like the verb होना and how to conjugate them into simple present tense, which is also called simple habitual tense. This way, you can practice some sentences, along with your vocabulary terms. I think this is the fastest and easiest way to learn Hindi vocabulary; especially, when you combine them with the flashcards, you should purchase, from indirectknowledge.com.

"So intransitive verbs in Hindi all end with ना. This is the root हो + ना, to make the intransitive verb होना. Here are some other intransitive verbs that are common.

To read पढ़ना

To speak बोलना

To write चाहना

To want चाहना

To come आना

To go जाना

To tell बताना

To think सोचना

To do करना

"These are common verbs used in everyday language Sarat. These should be learned from the start, since they will be useful for speaking, and interpreting the dialogues of others who communicate with you.

"To conjugate them into the simple present tense or what is also called the habitual present tense take the ना stem off each verb, and add ता, ती, or ते to the root.

"Let's look at how they would look.

Reads पढ़ता है

Speaks बोलता है

Writes चाहता है

Wants चाहता है

Come आता है

Goes जाता है

Tells बताता है

Thinks सोचता है

Does करता है

"I have added the ता stem now to these same verbs. I could have easily added ती or ते to indicate a particular gender association as well as singular or plural contexts. When these stems are applied they must match the gender of noun, and the appropriate verb ending for 'to-be' होना, i.e. हूं हैं है हो. Just like the हूं हैं है हो must match the singular or plural or the closeness or farness of an object, the verb stem must match as well.

"I know this sounds confusing, so let me share an example, and explain better.

Pronoun & Verb	Masculine	Feminine
They speak.	वे बोलते हैं।	वे बोलती हैं।

So you notice in the above example, that I have chosen the pronoun they, and the verb to speak (बोलना). The pronoun is referring to more than one person, so it is plural, and therefore requires nasalization, i.e. dot above the hang-bar, to match the plural in the pronoun. Also the verb बोलना; meaning 'to speak,' has dropped the intransitive stem ना and I've replaced it with the simple present stem ते and ती depending on if I'm talking to or about men or women, when referring to them.

"In Hindi ते references masculine nouns and pronouns; while ती references feminine nouns and pronouns. Masculine nouns and pronouns that are singular; meaning, that they are referencing only one person, place, or thing, are represented by the stem ता.

"For this reason, for every noun you learn, ever, you must learn whether it is a masculine noun or a feminine noun. This is very important, because the verb stems must correspond with each accordingly.

"So Sarat, you've learned a lot up to now. We'll take a break with the grammar, and now turn to the vocabulary terms you will memorize. I'll make a list for you, and then create a dialogue you might hear someone speaking, using the grammar and terms. Ready?" Sita asked him.

"Yes, Sita, I'm ready," Sarat gave as his reply.

"Okay, here's your list:

आदमी Man (m.)

औरत Woman (f.)

लड़का Boy (m.)
लड़की Girl (f.)
लोग People (m.)
गाली Abusive Language (f.)
दुर्घटना Accident (f.) [car accident, etc.]
हिसाब Maths (m.)
व्यक्ति Person/Individual (m.)
दोस्त Friend (m./f.)
दर्द Pain (m.)
परिचय Introduction/Acquaintance (m.)
अभिनेता Actor (m.)
अभिनेत्री Actress (f.)
वैसे Actually
पता Address (m.)
वयस्क Adult
फ़ायदा Advantage (m.)
सलाह Advice (f.)
लाभ Gain/Profit (m.)
सलाह Advice/Counsel/Tip (m./f.)
सलाह देना To advise/To preach/To counsel
हवाई जहाज़ Airplane (m.)

असर पड़ना To make a difference
काम Work (m.)
प्यार Affection
प्यार से Affectionately
से From/By/Of means of/As of/Since/Than
में At/ By/ For/ Within/ Inside/ On/ Among/ Under
को On [Can also mark a direct or indirect object]
स्नेह Love (m.)
के बाद Past/Beyond/Subsequent to/From __ on..
दोपहर Afternoon/Midday (m.)
बाद में Next/Then/After/Subsequently/Later on
दुबारा Again
फिर Again
फिर से Again
मानना To agree/To Accept
आगे Ahead

एक-जैसा Alike/The same
सब All/Everything/Everyone
सभी All
ठीक Okay/True/Right
रात भर All night
गली Alley (f.)
अकेला Alone
भी Also
पहलू aspect, side (m.)
विकल्प Alternative (m.)
क्योंकि Because
के कारन Because of/Due to/What with
और And/Also/Plus
अर्थ Meaning
मतलब Meaning
अनेकार्थी Ambiguous [Having more than one meaning]
प्रच्छन्न भाव Undertone (m.) [Hidden meaning/Intent]
छिपे अर्थ Undertone (m.) Hidden meaning/Intent]

तथापि Yet/However

के सात With/And all/Herewith/Together With/Along with

महान Great/Excellent/Famous/Noble

कुछ Some/Few

अच्छा Good/Fine/Kind/All right

"Sarat, now let's take some of these terms and use them in a random context, in the form of sentences. This will help you integrate the words in your mind better, while also giving you a starting point for creating some of your own sentence constructions. Here is are some random sentences for this lesson:

Hindi Sentences:

वे अच्छी हिंदी बोलते हैं| कुछ लोग यहां नहीं आते हैं| लड़का अच्छी तरह से लिखते हैं| लड़की बताती है. सूरत अच्छी तरह से पढ़ता है| अभिनेता सोचता है| अभिनेत्री सलाह देता है. सीता सलाह देता है| हिंदी शब्द अस्पष्ट हैं| मैं हिन्दी से

प्यार है. वह स्नेही है| सीता महान स्नेह के साथ सूरत से प्यार करता है| छिपे अर्थ क्या है?

English Sentences:

They speak good Hindi. Some people do not come here. The boy writes well. The girl tells. Sarat reads well. The actor thinks. The actress advises. Sita gives advice. Hindi words are ambiguous. I love Hindi. She is affectionate. Sita loves Sarat with great affection. What is the hidden meaning?

"Sarat ji, this completes our lesson for today. I only have one last mention to educate you on. In English there is what are called prepositions. In Hindi these are changed to postpositions. For example, 'For Prema...' would be 'Prema for...' or in Hindi प्रेमा के लिए. Another example would be the English sentence, 'Sarat is with only Sita,' would be in Hindi: 'सूरत ही सीता के साथ है|' Can you understand this? I can teach you more about this later, yet wanted to give you clarity, for when you are studying the sentences in this lesson," explained Sita.

"Sita I will take the lesson with me, and study intently. I shall learn this information as best I can, and hopefully be ready for another lesson soon," shared Sarat.

"Well then, this is the end of the lesson, and it is almost five o'clock. Nearly one hour has passed.

"Just let me know when you are ready for another lesson, and we'll arrange a time. Okay?" concluded Sita.

"Okay, I will. I should probably get back to the apartment now, and get ready for temple tonight. Thank you for the lesson, and understanding, Sita," said Sarat.

"Just take my advice and pray. God is in control and everything happens for a reason. Just pray," said Sita smiling affectionately at Sarat.

"Bye," said Sarat, heading out the door.

"Bye Sarat ji," said Sita.

In his car driving back to the apartment Sarat was on cloud nine again. He had at least shared his feeling, and now knew Sita's feeling toward him. He also was sharing something special with Sita; namely, learning Hindi.

Back at the apartment, Prema was cooking dinner, and helping Mitch with his homework. She was also instructing Michelle in the art of Indian vegetarian cuisine.

It seemed like everything going fine, which was surprising, when you think about it. Prema sort of took control, and took over in everybody's lives; however, strangely as it may sound, it seemed Michelle and Mitch were better off for it.

"Mitch how many time must I explain this to you. You must learn to pay attention better. This is why your teachers are fed up with you. Show and interest will you?" Prema scolded Mitch.

"I'm trying, but it is hard Prema," said Mitch.

"Focusing on how hard it is will only make it harder. Now you must take it in small doses. If you are not able to understand complex things, break them down yaar[1]," she insisted.

"In Algebra you must have heard of the FOIL method, yes?" she asked Mitch.

"FOIL method?" he questioned.

"First, Outer, Inner, Last, yaar! It is the acronym for the order of operations.

"You first start with what's first in the equation. Then what is on the outside. Then what is in the inside. Lastly what is last. This is how you know. Come on Mitch I will explain to you. It will make it so much easier," said Prema.

Prema worked with Mitch until he fully understood. He was very grateful for her help, but not for her attitude. He knew the only way to get her to leave him alone, was to actually learn what needed to be learned. His motivation was more to make her happy, than to pass the class.

"Michelle, now add just a small pinch of Hing[2]," instructed Prema.

"Like this?" Michelle asked her.

"Yes. Still less actually."

"Okay that is the right amount. Add that now," Prema said.

When Sarat walked in the apartment, the entire house smelt of deliciousness. He was hungry, but it was too late to eat, as everyone was dressed and ready to go to temple.

"What is for dinner?" asked Sarat.

"Never mind that now. Get a shower Sarat. It is time nearly to leave for temple. Hurry! Hurry!! Hurry!!!" demanded Prema.

Sarat didn't argue with her. He took a shower, put on a fresh dhoti and kurta, and walked back into the front room.

"Mitch? Michelle? You both are coming again to temple? What about your homework? What about not wanting to go to temple ever again? You both really have me confused," Sarat said.

"Sarat, let's go," said Prema.

"I would like some answers first please. What is going on?" he demanded.

"Sarat, all homework is done. Mitch knows his maths now, and Michelle can now cook sabji[3] biryani[4]. I have instructed them. No worries.

"As for temple, they know how important it is now to have spiritual knowledge as well as formal education. So they will come.

"Now can we please go? Please Sarat," she pleaded.

"Come let's go," said Sarat, trying to sound in control.

On the way to the temple, Prema asked Sarat, "How was your work dear?"

"Oh. It was a typical day really. I am still learning the job, but I am learning it well and competently," he shared with her.

"You are so brilliant Sarat. I am sure you make the best manager," said Prema.

In the back seat, Michelle and Mitch were laughing at Prema's compliment, and the funny manner in which she delivered it.

"Mitch? Michelle? What is so funny that you must share with everyone?" asked Prema.

"Nothing," blurted Mitch quickly.

"Is it really that funny that it should be nothing Mitch?" said Prema, holding her pointer finger up to show her disapproval that he was keeping secrets.

"It is silly really. Not worth repeating. Forgotten already Prema," said Mitch.

"No secrets or poking fun of anyone in this family Mitch. Do you hear me?" said Prema.

"Yes. I hear you. Sorry ma'am," said Mitch humbly.

"Michelle is now being quiet too. Let's be quiet the rest of the ride, shall we?" suggested Prema.

Nobody else said anything until they arrived at the temple, a short time later.

"Well we're here. Prema you should be happy, as we are early, like you wanted," said Sarat.

"I am happy for that, yes Sarat. You make me very happy," she said to him.

"Michelle, you look fantastic. Absolutely like a Hindu Goddess," remarked her brother Sarat, admiring her new Sari.

"Thank you Sarat," said Michelle, humbly, and smiling.

When all four of them entered the temple, they made their way to where Prema usually sat with her friends. Her friends hadn't quite arrived, so they all sat together chatting. Prema was explaining to them the significance of many gods and goddesses, and the many stories she knew about the pastimes of Lord Krishna. She was a great storyteller anyone would admit.

About ten minutes later Ahita arrived wearing her most beautiful sari. She wanted to impress not only Lord

Krishna, but also Mitch. She next to him, quietly as she listened in on Prema's stories.

"Prema, you are an excellent storyteller," commented Ahita.

"I have always been in love with Krishna, to the extent that I have studies all these pastimes of the Lord. This is the only reason I must be good at telling the stories," she said.

"None the less, you are gifted at telling these stories. Thank you for telling them," said Ahita.

"Ahita, you I like your sari. You look very beautiful," said Mitch, hoping nobody else would hear.

"Thank you Mitch," said Ahita quietly.

There was definitely some type of bond forming between Mitch and Ahita. They were acting very comfortable with each other, and she would only sit beside him, and no one else.

When the program started, Sita walked in. She glanced at Sarat and nodded. Prema noticed, but pretended not to. Sarat hoped she didn't notice. He didn't want any more drama than he already had.

After the program Sarat and Mitch were served once again prasadam by Prema and Ahita. Then sometime later, Prema asked Sarat if it would be okay if Ahita, Radha, and Siya, spend the night. Her spin was that they were going to have a girl's movie night, since tomorrow was Saturday, and so no school.

"I don't think that would be a good idea Prema?" said Sarat.

"Please Sarat. Michelle has already said we can stay in her room. I promise we'll be quiet, and not disturb you and Mitch. Please Sarat. We will be good, I promise you," said Prema.

"What about their parents though?" asked Sarat.

"They are all grown adults. They have already received permission from their parents however. Please Sarat, please!" she pleaded.

"Okay fine, but they should take another car, because mine will be too packed with people," he said.

"Ahita has a car. We will take hers," solved Prema.

When everyone arrived at the apartment, Prema instructed everyone to have a seat, while she and Ahita served everyone the sabji biryani Michelle and she had cooked.

"Guys have a big appetites. Mitch you and Sarat will eat all of this, even after eating healthy portions of prasadam at the temple.

"No worries though, we have cooked enough food for all of us, and even enough for you tomorrow to eat as you like.

"Sarat, are you working tomorrow or will you spend time with me?" asked Prema.

Sarat was off, but thought about the answer he wanted to give. Finally he just said honestly, "I am off work tomorrow."

Prema just smiled at him. She was brimming with loving affection for him. It was also difficult for him to not have some positive feelings toward her. She was after all helping him in so many ways, and had shown only care and concern for him and his family. Prema was a sweet girl, when she wanted to be. Certainly when she was getting her way she was happy.

After dinner, the girls shut themselves in Michelle's room and watched movies. They were as quiet as five girls could be. Sarat was just happy that Mitch and him could hang out alone and talk by themselves.

"Mitch, I'm sorry about everything with Prema," Sarat apologized.

"Actually, Prema is an acquired taste I think. She is actually a sweet, caring person, and even though she can be mean, it's out of concern and love I think. I don't know really, I have a hard time reading her. She's something else," judged Mitch.

"Well, I mean about forcing you to temple this morning, and this evening also," Sarat said.

"I didn't think I would like it, and definitely didn't like being forced to go, but I actually have a good time. It is a very spiritual place, and Ahita has taken me to be her boyfriend…I think," confessed Mitch.

"I think Ahita really likes you Mitch. How do you feel about her?" asked Sarat.

"I think I'm falling for her. Did you see how beautiful she looked tonight? She looks like a princess.

"Earlier we were talking and she was telling me how much she loves animals. She was also telling me how much Prema is crazy about you," said Mitch.

"She's crazy alright," said Sarat, laughing. Mitch started laughing too, thinking about it.

"I don't know. I don't want to hurt Prema, but I'm actually in love with another girl at the temple. I haven't introduced you to her, because Prema knows about her, and keeps me away from her completely.

"When dad got mad that I was away, I tried explaining how I could stay with her no more and this upset her. Then, I made the mistake of sharing all of that with Prema, and poof, what do you know, I have a crazy, insane, girlfriend, who has invaded my life.

"I really don't know what to do about it all. I like Prema, and don't want to hurt her, but I am really in love with the other girl. Please keep this between only you and me," said Sarat.

"You know me. I would never say anything. That's what brothers are for.

"Anyway, I guess things will work out for the best," said Mitch, trying to stay positive.

"I hope you're right!" said Sarat, turning out the lamp next to his bed. "Good night Mitch," he said.

"Night, Sarat," Mitch returned.

The next morning, all the girls were up taking turns taking showers. They were prettying each other up in Michelle's room, talking about boys, and sharing personal things with each other.

Sarat was still sleeping, but Mitch had awaken early. He wondered out into the front room to study some more on his school work. He was secretly hoping that Asha would come in and find him there. He wanted to spend as much time as he could with her, without others being around to listen in.

Prema finally found him out there studying, and commented that he was finally taking his studies serious. She also told him she was very proud of him. He smiled and thanked her.

"Ahita, Mitch is out here, why don't you make him some breakfast?" said Prema, loud enough that Mitch could hear her.

"That's okay Prema. She doesn't have to go to the trouble?" said Mitch.

"She wants to Mitch. Let her be happy, she will love you for it. She is sooooo in love with you. Lucky for you, aye?" said Prema.

"I like her too," said Mitch.

"Like her or love her? There is a difference you know," asked Prema.

"Love her," he confessed, knowing that if he said he only liked Ahita that it would get back to her, and she would be sad.

"Then you must tell her how you feel. Make it known to her, not me," suggested Prema.

"Wait I'll have her come talk to you," said Prema.

"Ah..." was all Mitch got out, before Prema was already in Michelle's room telling Ahita to come talk to him in the front room.

Soon Ahita arrived.

"You wanted to tell me something, Mitch?" she asked him.

"Ahita, I...I...I..." he couldn't get it out.

"Yes?" she asked him.

"I love you," said Mitch.

"I love you too," said Ahita.

"You do?" questioned Mitch, surprised.

"Mmm hmm" she said hummed, shaking her head slowly yes.

"Let me make breakfast, and I'll come get you when it's ready, okay?" she asked.

"Sure," said Mitch, smiling back at her. Feeling wonderful!

Love is something unpredictable. It happens when you least expect it, and most often at the most inconvenient times. It's bitter sweet.

Before long all the girls were in the kitchen, messing around. Siya was on one side of the counter, rolling out chapattis[5], and puris[6], with Michelle's help. While Ahita and Prema were talking about Mitch and Sarat; while one was preparing dal[7], at the same time as the other cut vegetables for what would be a remarkable Indian curry dish. Prema could stir up curry as easily as she could stir up trouble. She was good like that.

Notes

¹ Yaar is the Hindi slang word for the English equivalent of dude.

² Hing is Hindi for the Asafoetida. It is a replacement for garlic and onion in many devoutly religious Hindu homes, who do not believe it is good to eat garlic or onion.

³ Sabji is Hindi for vegetable.

⁴ Biryani is an Indian rice dish.

⁵ Chapattis are a common Indian flatbread, eaten with most daily meals.

⁶ Puris are a less common Indian deep fried bread that balloons up, and can be stuffed with dry vegetable dishes; commonly, potatoes and peas.

⁷ Dal is Hindi for lentils. When prepared correctly dal is a tasty rice accompaniment. It is common for Indian's to eat dal on a daily basis.

CHAPTER 5

Lord's Park

"Lord I pray to you for help. I am not knowing why things are as they are. I know I know so little. I turn my actions over to you and worship you in my heart.

"I should be non-attached to the outcomes of life; focused only on you, and delighting always in your majesty, oh Lord.

"These tears I cry, oh Lord, are for you my God. I cannot find happiness without your help, oh Lord. I want only to do what is right and just and dharmic.

"These two very different girls have my heart. One I am in love with, wanting to be with. She is completely attached to you, of Lord. The other is in love with me, seeing you only in me, oh Lord. She is a girl obsessed with me, just as Radharani was attached to you oh Lord.

"My selfish choice, where my heart takes me to in thought, is on the girl named Sita. I am married to her in my mind, as Rama was married to Sita in Ramayana.

"Oh Lord what am I to do? I know not! I need your help and guidance, and put my faith in you only, oh Lord.

"Please oh Govinda, Great Hari, Great Preserver Vishnu, I beseech you, I plead with you, make my heart want only you, and to do what is right and just, without hurting anyone.

"I...

An hour passed, and Sarat was strolling down the paths in Lord's Park, just down the road from his father's apartment in Elgin.

Lord's Park was 108 acres. There was a museum, a zoo, swimming facilities, and geese that he avoided, but observed with interest.

Sarat was seeing God in everything; his heart tender and emotions sensitive to everything going on inside him, as well as the natural beauty that was Lord's Park.

When he finished his prayer, he felt empowered, he felt better. He somehow felt that Lord Krishna was where he needed his focus to be. He had fallen into the trap that many sadhaks fall into; namely, forgetting their true nature.

Spirituality had become his feeling there that afternoon in the park. He had blocked out his troubles, his grief, the situations that were mere illusions, which were not real anymore in his mind.

Transcending this illusion, illuminated his mind to something less understood by people. People, actually most people, think their existence is something they control, or something they falsely believe is real, and it isn't.

Truth always has been. Nothing material lasts, and therefore is not really real. The effects of believing in something that is not real, can take us down the pages of a book and make us think we're really there, and the reality is we're never apart from the Lord of Truth.

Sarat was realizing this. It was building in him.

Eventually the sky went dark, and the Park became a cold oblivion, and he knew it was time to leave to leave and return to his illusion, and bring with it his newfound understandings.

A prayer. A single prayer. A prayer can be so powerful, like a seed that becomes a tree that lasts beyond human life. The truth of a prayer is something that cannot be denied, even by the atheist, because the observations of the results of prayers are as real as anything perceived.

A prayer in the park, Lord's Park, had transformed his worry, his fear, his heart's pain, and made him strong and a man. The boy he was, was timid and afraid; scared most of all of loss. He had lost his mother, his step-brother, his father, his brother and sister, Sita, and everyone and everything he'd ever known at one time or other along his life's journey. His heart had become cold on the outside, and weaker and weaker on the inside; but, this had all changed, in this afternoon, in Lord's Park—all because of a heartfelt prayer.

Walking back to the house, Sarat, took a deep breath, and let it out slowly, and shut his eyes for a temporary moment, and found the strength he would need to confront his controllers. He was determined to do the righteous thing now, and call the shots.

Opening the door to his father's apartment, we're Prema and her friends, his brother Mitch and sister

Michelle. They were all calm and everything was in order. The place felt like a different place altogether.

"Prema, I need to see you privately," said Sarat looking at her with a serious look.

Prema just sat there, and looked at him.

"Now please," said Sarat, making it clear that his need was more like an order.

Prema got up off the sofa in the front room, and followed him into Mitch's and his room.

"Yeah, what's up Sarat?" she asked lowering his eyes in expectation of him saying something hurtful.

"Prema, you have been a perfect friend in many ways. I cannot ever begin to tell you how much your friendship means to me. I have so much love for you—as a friend.

"I want you to always be my friend. As far as a relationship of romance, I want to suspend those ideas. We both need to focus on our obligations. I need to know you understand this," he shared.

"Sarat, I am in love with you," said Prema.

"I know this, Prema, I want you not to be in love with me. I love Sita, still," he added.

"My heart wants to break Sarat. Sarat, why do you hurt me so? Have I not done everything right? Have I not helped you? Have I not helped your family? Have I not been there for you?" she asked.

"You have been all those things. I am forever grateful of your friendship. I cannot lead you on. I must be honest with you, and share my true feelings," he said.

"Sarat!" she said, starting to cry.

"Prema, please do not make this difficult," he pleaded with her.

"How can I not?" she said.

"Prema, please, pray with me. I want you only to be happy, but I cannot make you happy indefinitely. I want infinite happiness for you. Please do not cry, dear Prema. Please do not cry one tear even," he said to her.

"Sarat, my heart hurts hearing these words. I want you to love me. Why does nobody love me?" she asked.

"You have so much love. My family loves you. I love you. Your friend's love in immeasurable. I just want you to understand my feelings, and keep yourself open to love, and not hate me for being honest," he said.

"Sarat, my heart is broken. You have broken my heart. You have broken my heart Sarat. My heart! Why couldn't you have broken Sita's heart? She doesn't even love you! Not the way that I love you Sarat," Prema said to Sarat, crying the tears of heartbroken young girl.

Prema left the room, and found Ahita and asked her to drive her home. Prema left.

"What did you say to her?" asked Michelle.

"Yeah, what did you say to make her cry Sarat?" asked Mitch, upset with his brother.

"I was honest," he said.

"You're a fool Sarat!" said Mitch.

"I cannot believe you hurt her like you did Sarat?" said Michelle.

"I cannot explain this to you two, but..." said Sarat.

"What is the matter with you? Do you not see how much she loves you? You two are perfect for each other," lamented Michelle.

"Just let me be," said Sarat, leaving their presence.

Love

Sarat left the house that night. It was hard explaining his predicament to his siblings. It was hard enough understanding his actions himself. Apart of him was really morning losing Prema. Prema had been a godsend when he needed her most. His heart was married to Sita however; something that couldn't be forgotten, or made to leave his mind.

Driving his car, directionless, and hearing his brother and sister's words replaying over and over in his head, he almost started believing a lie he wanted to believe.

It is hard to understand, dear reader, but Sarat did the right thing, the dharmic thing. He was honest. A quality most of us do not have when it matters most.

We let ourselves live the lie, and wonder always, what might have been. We die with our hearts broken, though we have people in our lives who love us beyond what we deserve. I know it is hard to understand. It was hard for me to understand too.

Pulling up to Sita's apartment, he got out of his car, and boldly walked the stairs to her apartment to claim his one true love. He was doing what he thought was the right thing to do.

"Sita, it is Sarat, let me in please," said Sarat, knocking on her door. It was seven-thirty at night.

Sita opened the door, and let him in. "Sarat, why are here?"

"For the same reason I should have refused to leave in the first place—I love you Sita"

"I love you, but what about Prema?" she inquired, with a hurt inflexion in her voice.

"I took your advice and prayed. I am doing what is in my heart right. I told Prema I did not love her, but as a friend. She left, upset, and will likely be upset for some time, yet I am not going to hurt you or her anymore. I love you Sita," he said.

"I love you too. I cannot believe you told her goodbye that easy. It must have hurt her a lot, don't you think?" Sita asked him.

"I surely must have, but I couldn't stand the thought of hurting you for one more minute, and lying to her about my feelings. It's not right," said Sarat.

"Are you and me together?" asked Sita.

"I think we've always been together," he said.

"How do you mean Sarat?" she asked confused.

"I mean I think we were born to be together, like Rama and Sita, the Divine Couple," he explained to her.

That night Sita was more emotional than usual. She had fallen in love with Sarat, finally. She had always kept herself at bay, away from the prospect of loving him, in that way, but when love befalls you, it befalls you.

In this story, Sita kept her distance. She allowed Sarat to live his life, and trusted God to make things right. She was a deeply religious girl of good character. She had a beautiful heart, but didn't show it to anyone. Sita had been hurt by everyone in her life. Her parents disowned her. She had run away to Chicago with seven-thousand nine-hundred dollars she had saved over two years, of living with her parents, as she worked as a cashier in a retail shop in Saint Louis.

The night she was kicked out, was the night after her graduation from high school. It was a devastating and emotionally depressing time in her life. She didn't trust people. She had a hard time getting close to people, because the people from her past had never really showed much attention or care or love for her. They found her to be an obligation, and a liability they didn't want.

Sita had not contacted them since the night she boarded an Amtrak train for Central Station in Chicago, leaving the Saint Louis station.

When she arrived she lived a few days in a hotel. Then a devotee from the temple took her in, and then later helped her get this seven-hundred dollar a month apartment in a not-so-good area. It wasn't far from the temple. And with some of her money she bought a midnight blue Chevy Celebrity, from another devotee selling it to upgrade to another newer auto.

Her money was running scarce, and she only had about twenty-three hundred left.

Sita didn't worry though. She was always believing that God would take care of her. Her God would be the only thing she would trust and love. She had read many Sanskrit texts, and had at one point considered becoming a renunciate, taking up sannyasa[1].

When she prayed about this, she received in a dream her dharma—to be a householder in India. It was what she knew was her destiny; yet, she relied on God to get her there, in the right time. Therefore she was preparing for the journey, by learning Hindi, and waiting for what needed to unfold to unfold.

"Sarat, let's pray," suggested Sita.

"We should," he agreed.

Sita took Sarat over in front of her alter, and together they prayed for dharma to prevail, and for them to trust in God for everything to work out for the best.

Then Sita made Sarat a pallet on the floor, and they went to sleep. At three o'clock Sita awoke and woke Sarat, and they picked up where they had left off, before Prema entered the picture, or Sarat had the issues with his father.

When they arrived at the temple together, in Sita's car, Sarat took a deep breath. He didn't want a confrontation, or to see anyone hurt. He wanted only that all the devotees should be happy, devoutly worshiping God, and for God to make things well.

"सूरत आप तैयार[2] हैं?" Sita asked Sarat.

"मैं तैयार सीता हूँ।" he replied her.

"तो मुझे अंदर ले लो।" Sita said.

"आज मैं आप के साथ बैठेंगे, सीता आओ। चलो चलते हैं," कहा सूरत।

When Sarat took Sita inside the mandir, they sat together where Sita generally had been sitting. Prema was there, sitting in the company of her girlfriends.

Just before the morning program began, Mitch and Michelle entered the temple, and took a seat next to Prema. She was smiling when they sat beside her. Sarat, wondered why they came, but never said anything to them during the program; nor did they say anything to him either.

"सूरत, अपने भाई और बहन यहाँ हैं," सीता मुस्कुराते हुए कहा।
And that was that. For now.

After the program was finished, Sita served Sarat prasadam, and sat with him at a table alone, sheltered from the others. She understood that it would take time to heal the hurt endured by Prema, and it wasn't her intention to flaunt victory.

Nearly finished eating, Sarat's brother came to their table, and Sarat introduced Mitch to Sita. Mitch acted kind, and after sitting down, said, "Sarat, Prema told me to tell you, 'Please let's end the cold shoulder, come over and join our table, please,' so Sita and you should come and join us. Please feel welcome!"

"सीता मेरे साथ आओ?" सूरत पूछा।
"मैं निश्चित रूप से आप के साथ सूरत आ जाएगा," सीता ने कहा।
"This is good. This is really good," said Mitch, excited.

Sarat stood, then did Sita, and they followed Mitch over to Prema's table, and she asked them to all take a seat.

"Sarat, I was very badly hurt last night. Even this morning I was upset terribly. I almost didn't come to the mandir today, because I didn't want to face you.

"I see now that you truly love Sita. I was jealous of her, because I wanted you.

"Sita I am sorry for the way I have behaved in the past. I see now that you are devoted to Sarat, and I see you love him very much. He is very lucky to have you.

"Sarat, cannot be mad anymore. I want only your friendship, and Sita's friendship, if she will be my friend, and for both of you happiness.

"I realize you were being honest with me last night. I didn't want to believe your honesty, but I thank you for it. I pushed myself on you, and I told you things in hopes that you would forget Sita, and only think of me.

"Love does not work that way. No one knows this more than me. Please forgive me, both of you, and let's be friends and forget this matter. Can we?" asked Prema.

"Prema you have a kind heart, it will be hard for any man not to love you that is not already in love. You are great friend, and have been a blessing in my life, and my family's life, and I will never be able to repay you for this love you have shown me. I am fortunate beyond what I deserve. Accept my apology also, and know that I will always love you as a friend. Nothing can ever take this away from us. There is nothing for you to apologize for, and all that was is in the past, is in the past. Accept my apology for hurting you with honesty. Honesty kills more hearts than the good it does, but that is the nature of honesty, and why many people forget their true nature and sacrifice love for a lie," said Sarat.

"Prema, I know it must have been difficult hearing those words of Sarat's last night. Any girl would have been upset, and hurt by those words. Sarat really didn't mean to hurt you, and it wasn't his intention to do so. He confided this to me, and I know it hurt him hurting you. I can tell he cares about you very much. I want to be your friend. Please accept my friendship, and I will love you like my best friend," said Sita.

The rest of the hour was spent sharing laughter and stories. Mitch and Michelle had become devout in their wish to be there, and they had only Prema to thank for that.

Prema recounted the story of how her and Mitch were at odds with each other, and Sita commented, "Mitch met his match, did you not Mitch?" she asked looking at him.

"Hindu girls rule!" said Prema, nudging Mitch.

Mitch just let her have her fun.

Michelle shared the story of how Prema had taught her how to cook Indian food.

"I will come over again today, and teach you more what to cook," commented Prema.

"I can hardly wait," said Michelle smiling at her.

It was a good day.

Mitch spent the better part of the day moving his belongings into Sita's apartment. She helped him, and at some point started cooking their afternoon meal.

Then by four o'clock, they returned to the mandir, and began practicing their Hindi.

Lesson 5

"Sarat, I must hold you accountable for your Hindi. As I said before, you must master each lesson before going on to the next. Therefore I will give you a test, to see how well you have mastered the language. Remember, always remember, actually, that the truest test of mastery of a language is how flexible you are with the lessons you have learned, and how well you can apply your lessons in original conversations with others.

"This is one reason I have not developed dialogues that you can remember, but rather will give you sentences you can study, and practice, and arrange linguistically as you feel fit.

"Ready for the test?" Sita asked Sarat.

"Ready ji," he said.

Again he passed the test with flying colors.

"Okay, today I will teach you another lesson, and together with the last you can integrate them together in your mind, and let your lessons start becoming more unconscious for you, so that you can speak without thinking about what to say—you'll just know.

"The first part of this lesson I want to teach you about questions.

"Questions, first of all, follow English in the sense that they can rely on intonation to insinuate that they are a question. In Hindi, as in English, and upward inflection at the end of a sentence denotes a question.

"Next the words for what, where, when, why, and who are specific for Hindi as well; namely, क्या, कहाँ, कब, क्यों, कौन.

Notice that they all begin with क. This might make them easier to remember. It did for me.

"Yes or No questions just add क्या to the front of a sentence. Informally it is sometimes, and can be, added to the end of a sentence. It never gets added to the middle of a sentence for Yes or No questions, Sarat.

"Consider the sentence: आप हिंदी बोलते हैं| If you add क्या to the front it becomes a Yes or No question (e.g., क्या आप हिंदी बोलते हैं?). Pretty easy right?" she asked Sarat.

"Simple ji!" he exclaimed.

"Yes, and certainly you could say it without the क्या so long as you gave an upward inflection at the end of that declarative sentence.

"So the next point to teach is where the question-word goes if you are not asking a Yes or No question. The answer is just before the verb. For example the declarative statement: मंदिर है| We find that the verb is है. If we want to ask where the temple is, we use the Hindi word for 'where' which is 'कहाँ' would go just before the verb है. So it would read: मंदिर कहाँ है?

"यह मिल गया?" Sita asked Sarat.

"तुमने क्या कहा?" he replied.

"I'm saying colloquially, 'Do you have this?'" said Sita.

"Then the answer is 'Yes,'" he said.

"अच्छा" she said.

"So the next part is learning commands or requests. You'll need to learn this to be successful, living in India. You're always in situations where you need to make a request. Even here in America.

"Questions were easy, commands and requests are easy too!

"In Hindi you need to understand that there are regular and irregular verbs. Both have verb stems that change depending on the formalness of the communication. In Hindi there is an honorific system of communication. How old someone is, or what their status in life it, may require you to be more honorific and formal, or less.

"Regular verbs are easy you just add the stem: इयेगा for most formal contexts, इये for very formal contexts ओ for casual contexts, no ending at all for very informal contexts. So the verb to settle down in Hindi is: आराम से बैठना, if you take off the stem ना, you're left with आराम से बैठ, right?" she asked Sarat.

"Right," he replied.

"If you are asking your boss to settle down, knowing full well he has a higher place of authority than you do, you might politely say: आराम से बैठियेगा। If you're talking to a grandparent, who is irate, you might step it down to: आराम से बैठिये। If you're talking to your child, informally, you might say, आराम से बैठो। If you're upset with your young child and you're irate, you may command them to: आराम से बैठ!

"Now let me tell you about irregular verbs, because they are a bit different. There are four very common irregular verbs you'll use all the time; namely: to give, i.e. देना; to take, i.e. लेना; to do, i.e. करना; and to drink, i.e. पीना. These get conjugated a little differently. Here's how:

Situation	to give	to take	to do	to drink
Most Formal	दीजियेगा	लीजियेगा	कीजियेगा	पीजियेगा
Very Formal	दीजिये	लीजिये	कीजिये	पीजिये
Casual	दो	लो	करो	पियो
Informal	दे	ले	कर	पी

"So very similar, but note the changes with these four, because they are used so often. Sarat, if you want to negate a command there are two words to know. One is न and the other is मत. For the most formal and very formal uses use न just before the verb. For more casual and informal contexts, use मत just before the verb. Easy enough eh?" asked Sita.

"Quite simple, Sita!" said Sarat, keeping pace nicely.

"One last point about commands and request. When you're wanting someone to do something at some point in the future, or to show that you're not in a big hurry, or that you're not impatient, you can simply use the stem ना, in place of a the other conjugations. Like for instance if you want someone to go home some time tomorrow, you can say, कल घर कुछ समय जाना|

"Sarat, now I want to cover something else basic, and then I'll give some vocabulary, and sentences to study, sound good?" asked Sita.

"Sounds great!" he replied.

"Okay, so what I want to discuss now are nouns, adjectives, and how gender is used.

"So we'll start with nouns. Masculine nouns that end in अ change the ending ए to make the noun plural. If the noun doesn't end in अ then no change is made.

"Feminine nouns which end in ई or इ change their ending to इयां; while feminine nouns that do not end in ई or इ you add एँ to make them plural.

"Moving to adjectives, just know that they have to agree with the gender and number of what they are describing. In other words the noun that they are describing.

"A masculine noun will have a masculine adjective. The rule of thumb is that adjectives that end in आ inflect. A masculine noun that is singular, ending in अ simply stays the same. If it is singular, simply add ए. Feminine nouns that are plural simply end in ई. Some nouns can be both masculine and feminine and in these cases simply stick to the masculine stem. If you don't know the gender, it is best to stick to the masculine stem.

"Last point to make is that adjectives can come either before or after the nouns they modify. Knowing this gives you greater versatility. As in the English sentence 'The dog is yellow,' can also be said, 'This is a yellow dog'; the same applies in Hindi as well. So either: 'कुत्ते को पीला है|' or 'यह एक पीला कुत्ता है|'; never mind the postposition को in the first sentence, and how the adjective changes to plural. We will discuss postpositions more in depth in another lesson.

"Okay so this is the grammar. Not too bad eh?" asked Sita.

"It seems fairly straight forward," said Sarat.

"So let me give you some vocabulary words, and then some sentences, and you can practice this lesson.

Vocabulary Terms

कृपया Please
बैठो Sit
आप You
के लिए For
कुछ Some
शब्द Word
तुम्हें You
खुश Happy
होना Be, Happen, Take Place, Occur
चाहता Want
अब Now
केवल Only
अपनी Its, One's own
दोस्ती Friendship
चाहता है Wants

मुझे Me
प्यार Love, Affection, Devotion
करने Do
के लिए For
स्वतंत्र Free, Independent, Chainless
मुक्त Free
भरोसा Trust, Reliance, Hope, Indoctrination
जब When, As
जीवन Life, Soul
सुंदर Beautiful
जाता है Is, Are
मुझे Me
आओ Come
सिखाना होगा Will teach
भगवान God
भाषा Language
में In
जुड़ते Connect
ज्यादा More, Much
जानने Learn
अधिक More
हमारे Our, Ours
कोई Some, Certain (adjective) / Someone, Anybody, All (pronoun)
अवरोध Barrier

कर रहे हैं Are
से From, Of, By, To, Since, By Means Of
विशेषण Adjective
रंग Color
क्रिया Action
कार्रवाई Action
करने में In
मदद Help
संज्ञा Noun
इच्छाओं Desire, Wish
वस्तुओं Objects
की Of (preposition), How (conjunction)
वस्तुओं Object, Objective
जानें Learn more
अच्छी Good
तरह से Kind
अध्ययन Study
गर्व Proud
करते हैं Do

"Saratji, Here are some random sentences for you to examine and make sense of and be able to learn from. You'll be able to look at many key points from today's lesson, as well as previous lessons. There are even some introduction to future lessons.

"My preference in teaching is to provide you with an integrated approach that builds on the foundation material I have already given you, while also exposing your Other Mind (Unconscious Mind) to material you'll be anchored to and recognize intuitively in future lessons. This holistic approach works best, because it keeps you from under or over analyzing things to consciously or unconsciously.

"Looking back at what you've learnt already, you've come a long way so far in your Hindi lessons. You don't even know it yet, but you will soon as we dive into deeper waters with these lessons.

"Follow your heart with your learning, while at the same time let your mind be fixed on learning as well. If you have any doubt still about your ability to learn Hindi, I would encourage you to suspend your disbelief and see what happens," said Sita.

सूरत कृपया बैठो. प्रेमा आप के लिए कुछ शब्द है. वह तुम्हें खुश होना चाहता है. वह अब केवल अपनी दोस्ती चाहता है. अब आप सूरत मुझे प्यार करने के लिए स्वतंत्र हैं. प्यार मुक्त है. आप कृष्ण भरोसा जब जीवन आप के लिए सुंदर हो जाता है. मुझे सूरत आओ, मैं तुम्हें हिंदी सिखाना होगा. आप हम भगवान की भाषा में जुड़ते हैं, ज्यादा जानने के लिए अधिक हिन्दी. हमारे प्यार सूरत कोई अवरोध कर रहे हैं. मैं आप सूरत से प्यार है.

विशेषण हमारी भाषा रंग. क्रिया हमें कार्रवाई करने में मदद. संज्ञा हमारी इच्छाओं की वस्तुओं रहे हैं. हिंदी सूरत जानें. अच्छी तरह से अध्ययन करें. मुझे गर्व करते हैं.

Notes

[1] "The giving up of activities that are based on material desire is what great learned men call the renounced order of life [sannyasa]. And giving up the results of all activities is what the wise call renunciation [tyaga]." Bhagavad Gita 18:2

[2] तैयार is the Hindi word for 'ready' or 'prepared'.

CHAPTER 6

ऐसा कहा जाता है

There is a secret some people know; and, most other's do not. It is the knowing you know someone has you've met for the first time, where they smile at you, and accept you, and somewhere in that smile is a Truth you sense, but do not know. A truth that resides inside of them. A truth you yearn for in a single instant, and forget in a fleeting moment passing. It is a secret that guides their decisions, their determination to be great, and their abilities to overcome obstacles. It is an inner drive that is backed by a force greater than themselves. It is a faith that supersedes what most believe is possible, and it is a secret that sees them through their entire life. It is a secret called Dharma[1].

When a sadhaka[2] experiences this Truth they are liberated from the bondage of this material body; freed from Samsara, forever. Knowing ones calling is not always an easy thing to know, but when you know it, you know it, and you never forget it. Sita knew hers, and Sarat, doing regular sadhana with her, was bound to be in alignment with knowing his as well.

Greatness comes to you, you don't have to come to it. It is your divine birth rite. Man creates order, God destroys it, because it is not true order, but a fabrication of the True Order. Some people are afraid to wake-up and experience the Truth. When they muster the courage, tears will fall, and their entire being will vibrate and the sensations of Goosebumps will cover their entire body. An emotional upheaval happens, and something changes them in a fraction of a second. They're never the same. I've seen it happen time and time again. I am addicted, you might say, to watching it happen. Uniting with the divine is a site to see, if you know what to look for that is.

"Sarat, will you recite with me this morning the Lalita Sahasranama. I will help you," asked Sita.

"Yes," said Sarat.

It was the most beautiful sound you ever heard. The devotion was infused into the Language of God, and only a few mantras into the Sahasranama, both devotees began crying tears of intense love and devotion. It was pure love for God.

Each mantra Sita helped him with, took them deeper and deeper into a state of godliness. This was a religious hymn that had been recited through the ages many millions of times and here and now it was being recited with just as much devotion as anyone had ever recited it.

After doing sadhana the young couple, left for the mandir, where they joined Prema, Siya, Ahita, Mitch and

Michelle to worship Lord Krishna in loving unbroken devotion. For the pure hearted devotees perfect moments were when they were in the company of Lord Krishna; to the extent they only wanted to see and worship Krishna in every activity of every moment of every day.

"सूरत हम मंदिर और पूजा में पूरे दिन रहने के लिए और हिंदी का अध्ययन कर सकते हैं? यह पूजा यहाँ रहने के लिए इस तरह के एक संपूर्ण दिन की तरह लगता है," सीता ने उस से पूछा|

Sarat, agreed. They stayed all day. When they arrived back at the apartment it was nearly eight-thirty at night. Sita suggested they get some sleep, and so they did. Her reasoning was that Sarat had work tomorrow. He was now paying all the bills, and ensuring that they were saving money for India.

There were things Sarat didn't know, which he'd find out later, but we'll get to that as the story goes.

The next morning was much as the last, and the one before that, and the one before that, and…well…the ones before that as well. It was an extremely regulated way of life. It worked for the couple though. Some readers' may find the thought of this type of lifestyle incredibly boring and meaningless, but I suppose others would disagree. It is, or isn't, depending on the choice you make. It's up to you how you live your life.

In the morning Sarat awoke first, and nudged Sita awake. It was the first time he had awoken before her. She smiled when she saw his face over hers. It was pleasant waking up to the site of the man she loved.

"सीता आओ| तुम्हारी उन खूबसूरत आंखों को जगाने, और फिर दिन को पूरा करने का समय| पहले स्नान जाना है और मैं बाद में में कूद जाएगा," सूरत अपने एक सच्चे प्यार को प्यार से कहा, मुस्कुरा|

Sita got ready, and Sarat followed, and together a new day became their day together. After the morning program, Sarat went to work, and worked hard he did. He was growing into the position of manager well. It was sort of a dichotomy really in that he was detached from his work, yet worked as if he was completely devoted to it and only it. His devotion was actually to God; not the work per se.

After his work day ended he drove back to the mandir, where Sita was waiting for him.

Lesson 6

"Ready for another Hindi lesson, Sarat?" she asked him.

"Actually, I am ready Sita," he told her.

"I will not test you today, but please make sure you are always prepared by understanding the former lessons before proceeding to the next lesson. I know I sound like a broken record, but it is for your own good," said Sita.

"I will do as you instruct, Sita," he assured.

"Today's lesson I want to teach you about postpositions. Think about in English how sometimes, Sarat, we change from I to me, and my can change to mine. This is called inflection. In Hindi pronouns, nouns, and adjectives inflect as well. I am going to break this lesson into two parts so you can digest each part fully without being overwhelmed.

"So the first section is on singular nouns and pronouns. When a masculine noun is followed by a postposition, and happens to end in आ the noun takes on the plural ए ending. The same applies to adjectives which modify the noun. They also take on the ए ending. Pronouns, which, as you have learned never end in आ; will, however, inflect accordingly:

	का	को	से	में	पर
मैं	मेरा	मुझको	मुझसे	मुझमें	मुझपर
तू	तेरा	तुझको	तुझसे	तुझमें	तुझपर
यह	इसका	इसको	इससे	इसमें	इसपर
वह	उसका	उसको	उससे	उसमें	उसपर
हम	हमारा	हमको	हमसे	हममें	हमपर

तुम	तुम्हारा	तुमको	तुमसे	तुममें	तुमपर
आप	आपका	आपको	आप से	आप में	आप पर
ये	इनका	इनको	इनसे	इनमें	इनपर
वे	उनका	उनको	उनसे	उनमें	उसपर
कौन (S.)	किसका	किसको	किससे	किसमें	किसपर
कौन (PL.)	किनका	किनको	किनसे	किनमें	किनपर
कोई	किसी का	किसी को	किसी से	किसी में	किसी पर

"The first postposition का inflects, but the other postpositions do not. This special postposition is similar to the English apostrophe '<u>s</u> in that it contrasts ownership. For example, in English we might say: 'This is Michael's bag!' In Hindi we would state it as, 'यह माइकल के बैग है!' Notice that के is inflecting the noun बैग it modifies.

"The next postposition को means 'to' or 'of' and can take on other instances for which it is used, which I'll get to later. For example, 'Tonight we dance in the moonlight,' in Hindi would read: 'रात को हम चांदनी में नृत्य.'

"The next postposition से, usually means from, but can also be used as: at, by, off, of, with, as of, by means of, etc. Take the sentence: From her Sarat learned many things. In Hindi this could be said: 'उससे सूरत बहुत कुछ सीखा|'

"The next postposition is में which means 'in'. In English we say, 'I live in my house.' In Hindi we say, 'मैं अपने घर में रहते हैं|'

"The next postposition पर is often used in the context of 'at'; however, can be used to mean: on, down, upon, over, onto, etc. If you want to explain that, 'He shouted at her,' in Hindi you can say, 'वह उस पर चिल्लाया|'

"Sarat, let's transition now into the second part of this lesson. I want to now teach you about plural nouns and how to add postpositions to them. I also will cover with you postposition noun and pronoun contractions. Lastly, I'll talk to you about pronoun-noun-adjective combinations when used with postpositions.

"So let's begin with plural nouns. Take the singular noun boy, which becomes boys in the plural form. In Hindi we लड़का as the singular, and लड़के as the plural form. Now, we've said, earlier, that with a postposition a singular noun that ends in आ takes the plural forms stem ए when used with a postposition. So लड़के से means: from one boy. Still singular, because of the postposition. So how do we make it plural? Well, what we do is take the ए and replace it with ओं; hence, it become लड़कों से. Sarat, you can do this whether the noun ends in आ or ए. For example the noun मकान; meaning 'home' will change to मकानों से/में. We do this for all masculine nouns. The adjectives will not follow suite but stay the same as they do for the singular adjectives, having ए for the ones ending in आ.

"For feminine nouns that end in इयाँ change to इयों. For feminine nouns that end in एँ change to ओं when followed by a postposition. For example, लड़कियां changes to लड़कियों. Just like किताबें changes to किताबों.

"Now the postposition को which is very frequently used, is contracted to the pronoun preceding it, as we've learnt. There is another less formal or academic way of constructing and contracting them. Note this list:

Proper	Casual	Informal
मुझको	मुझे	मेरे को
तुझको	तुझे	तेरे को
इसको	इसे	
उसको	उसे	

हमको	हमें	हमारे को
तुमको	तुम्हें	तुम्हारे को
इनको	इन्हें	
उनको	उन्हें	
किसको	किसे	
किनको	किन्हें	

"Sarat, if you read newspapers or books and find these varying forms of representing the postposition को you'll find that you start to consciously recognize them without even thinking about it. In fact, I have some Bollywood movies we can watch tonight, which are in Hindi, and perhaps you can notice people speaking both forms. Watching and listening to Hindi language films will help your Hindi dramatically. It is one of the next best things to full immersion into the culture and country of India.

"So often we hear pronouns being used emphatically along with the nouns they represent. We might say, Sarat,

'From those people lots of things were learned.' In Hindi we can do the same thing. We actually do it the exact same way. In Hindi the same sentence would be said: 'उन लोगों से बहुत सी बातें सीखा रहे थे.' So instead of उनसे we have split the post position से away from the pronoun to insert the noun लोगों; hence 'उन लोगों से', transcribing and translating to 'From those people,' because they are not only people, but emphatically—*those* people!

"Sarat, this lesson may take some time to master. Let me now give you some vocabulary and some sentences to study along with the grammar lesson. I want you to remember this, the lesson is not as difficult as it may seem. Look at it expansively. Overall it is simple," said Sita.

"I am finding it easy to learn Hindi, the way you teach it Sita. तुम एक अच्छे शिक्षक हैं," said Sarat.

"Yes we've started in small measure, looking at the alphabet, then the words, then sentences, then paragraphs, then more; yet, keep in mind that by the time you are communicating fluently, you are already unconscious of all of this, using it brilliantly. The more you practice and use Hindi, the more affluent and natural it becomes. Do not worry about making mistakes, everyone does, even the best Hindi speakers. So have fun, and no worries!"

"I will take this advice to heart," commented Sarat.

"Okay, here are your terms to memorize:

घर home (m.)

अब now

में in
चल रहा हूँ running
नीले blue
दोस्त friend
जीवन life (m.)
के बाहर beyond, out of, outside
और and, more
अधिक more, further
चाहता है wants
अगर if
प्यार में in love
तो so, then
सभी everything, all
रंग color, hue
चमक brightness, shine, glow
फूलदान vase (for flowers)
फूल flower, bloom (m.)
डाल दिया put
गोवा Goa
लड़कियों girls
किसी one, a [human]

जगह place, (f.)
फूलदान vase
रात night
आग में in fire
उज्जवल bright
शीघ्र early, prompt
ही only, very [emphatic]
जाएगा will
नई new
शर्ट shirt (in English)
पर on, at, upon, via
अंत end
सिर head
कि that, if, so that, in order that
सुंदर beautiful
उसे her, him
साड़ी sari
कृत्रिम artificial, synthetic
निद्रावस्था hypnotic
उसकी his, her
विनम्रता humbleness, humility, delicacy

भगवान God
आता है comes
सुबह से morning
रात तक till the night
तक to, until, by
सोचता है thinks
के साथ with, together, accompanied, including
गिर fall
गई has been
दुनिया world
पूरी complete
तरह way
बदल change
भाग part
जा रहा हूँ I am going to
वहीं that's where
अभी भी still
किया जाएगा will be
मैंने I
कहा said

सही right, correct, unquestionable, true

"Sarat here are some random practice sentences using the vocabulary words, to give some context to how they can be used:

मैं घर जा रहा हूँ.

मैं अब घर में चल रहा हूँ.

मैं एक नीले कंप्यूटर है.

मेरे दोस्त जीवन के बाहर और अधिक चाहता है.

अगर आप प्यार में हैं, तो सभी रंग चमक रहे हैं.

मैं फूलदान में फूल डाल दिया.

वह गोवा से है.

लड़कियों के किसी और जगह से कर रहे हैं.

रात को आग में उज्जवल है.

वे शीघ्र ही यहाँ हो जाएगा.

मैं एक नई शर्ट पर है.

हिन्दी अंत में मेरे सिर में है.

यह है कि यह क्या है.

उसे सुंदर साड़ी कृत्रिम निद्रावस्था है.

उसकी विनम्रता भगवान से आता है.

सूरत सुबह से रात तक हिंदी के बारे में सोचता है.

सूरत सीता के साथ प्यार में गिर गई, तो उसकी दुनिया पूरी तरह से बदल दिया है.

मैं अब घर से बाहर भाग रहा हूँ.

मैं घर जा रहा हूँ.

मैं अभी भी वहीं सीता किया जाएगा.

मैं अभी वहाँ हो जाएगा कि मैंने कहा.

मैं यह सही कहा. हाँ?

"Also, to help you, here is an English translation:

I am going home.

I am walking in the house now.

I have a blue computer.

My friend wants more out of life.

When you are in love, then all colors are brighter.

I put the flowers in the vase.

She is from Goa.

The girls are from some place else.

At night fire is brighter.

They will be here shortly.

I have on a new shirt.

Hindi is in my head finally.

It is what it is.

Her beautiful sari is hypnotic.

Her humbleness comes from God.

Sarat thinks about Hindi from morning to night.

When Sarat fell in love with Sita, then his world changed completely.

I am running out of the house now.

I am leaving home.

I will be right there Sita.

I will be right there I said.

I said it right. Yes?

"Sarat, study this lesson, for some time and then we'll go back to our place and watch a Hindi movie. I will make us some pop-corn, and we'll have a date night in," said Sita.

"यह मुझे अच्छा लगता है!" सूरत कहा|

This is exactly what the young couple did.

Notes

[1] Dharma is religious duty or calling. It can also translate to mean Law of God.

[2] Sadhaka is a spiritual aspirant, devoted to religious duty.

CHAPTER 7

सम्मोहित किया

Repetition, repetition, repetition, it is enough to hypnotize someone. A day goes by. A week goes by. Then a month. Then it's March.

Sarat and Sita had been doing the same thing, every day, day and night, week after week, and they had gotten into a routine: It's awaken. It's bathe. It's pray. It's temple. It's work. It's Hindi. It's temple. It's prasadam. It's Hindi. It's home. It's sleep. It's repeat. Now it was March. Mitch had an *A* in all his classes. Prema's help helped him immensely.

These days Prema was at Sarat's dad's place more than he was. Mitch and Ahita were together; an item, you might say, though not officially. Michelle was engaged in the friendship she had with Prema, Siya, and Ahita. They were all close and spent most of their time together at one or the others homes.

It is amazing what happens when you make more money than you spend. Sarat now had $6,723.95 saved. Sita wouldn't let him spend money on anything except the bare essentials. They lived a very, let me emphasize, VERY simple life. Simple living and high thinking, had its rewards, however; namely, more money, more precious time enjoying each other's company, and plenty of time to engage in spiritual practice.

People change. Everyone did.

Sarat's dad had met someone. Her name was Kelly, and she was the first woman John had been with or dated since Sarat's mom had left the picture.

Kelly was good for him too. She liked traveling, and was now his partner on the road. She did the bookwork, and kept him fed. He drove the miles. John also liked that Kelly was a great communicator, and was excellent at talking to warehouse personnel and talking them into letting John unload and load quickly. Her charms were likeably useful.

The only difference between John being on the road now and before he had met Kelly is that now he was gone for even longer stints at a time. This was barely noticeable by his kids, because they were so engaged in their own lives these days.

"Mitch how well did you do on that exam in Math today?" asked Ahita.

"I think I did well," he said to her.

"Mitch thinking and doing are two different activities, two different activities—two different verbs," said Prema.

"What do you mean?" he asked Prema.

"I mean did you or didn't you ace it?" asked Prema.

"I aced it," he said, giving her a look.

"I hope so for your sake. I don't want to find out you make any less than an A on any paper or exam. You better keep that A," she threatened him.

"Prema lay off," I aced it, I'm sure.

"Mitch don't talk to her like that. She only wants to help you," said Ahita.

Prema was looking upset at him. Faking probably.

"Mitch apologize to Prema. You hurt her feeling," demanded Ahita.

"Mitch you are so mean sometimes," said Siya, chiming in on him too.

"Mitch you should be thanking Prema for her help," said Michelle, chiming in too.

Mitch could not hold his own with any of the girls one-on-one; let alone all four at once. He knew he wouldn't get any peace of mind until he apologized. He hated apologizing, yet hated having all of them ganging up on him at the same time. He knew the worst of the two evils was to not apologize, or else he wouldn't have.

"I'm sorry Prema. Prema I am so sorry. Everyone is right, I am so foolish, and I owe all thanks to you. Please forgive me. Please Prema," said Mitch, overdoing it.

Ahita poked his side.

"Okay! No. Seriously. I am very grateful for your help. I am sorry. I was smart-alecky, and I'm sorry for that too. You are right, I must make all A's," said Mitch, more sincerely.

"Alright then. I will help you after dinner. We'll study all night," she said, knowing it wasn't what he wanted to hear, smiling slyly.

"All night?!" he asked.

"All night buster!" she said, giving a serious look.

"Thank you Prema for helping him," said Ahita.

"No worries. I'll see to it that he graduates with an A for sure," said Prema. She was intent on keeping her word.

"I'm starving," said Mitch.

"You'll have to wait buster!" it won't be ready for some time.

Mitch figured he was being punished, but the truth is it just wasn't ready. Cooking Indian food is a time consuming job. Even for cooks like Prema.

Ring. Ring. Ring. Rang Mitch's cell phone.

"Hello," he answered.

"Mitch, it is Sarat."

"Hey ji!" said Mitch.

"He brother, I was wondering if was okay if Sita and I stop in for dinner tonight and hang out some," said Sarat.

Mitch knew he might not have to study all night, if Sarat and Sita came over, so he said, "Yes. You can come."

"Is Michelle cooking?" Sarat asked Mitch.

"Actually, Prema is over with the girls, and they are all cooking something up.

"Let me put her on the phone. You can ask her if you can come," said Mitch handing the phone to Prema.

"This is Prema," said Prema, grabbing the phone away from Mitch.

"Namaste Prema. It is Sarat. I was wondering if Sita and I could stop in for dinner. Mitch said you, Siya, Ahita, and Michelle were cooking over there tonight," said Sarat.

"Can I talk to Sita?" she asked him.

"Sure," said Sarat, handing the phone to Sita.

"Namaste! This is Sita."

"Sitaji, you and Sarat can come, but I was wondering if you could bring a dish also?" asked Prema.

"Yes of course. I will bring something, no worries. What time should we arrive?" asked Sita.

Prema was looking at Mitch, when she said, "How about eight o'clock. You two can stay the night if it gets too late."

Mitch's face dropped. It was only barely after five o'clock. Three hours was a long time to wait when you're starving.

"That sounds great. Thank Prema," said Sita.

"Okay then, see you," said Prema.

They hung the phone up.

"What's the deal asked Sarat?"

"The deal is we're eating over there at eight o'clock. This means I'll have plenty of time to make my sabji korma. Awesome!" said Sita.

"Oh that's a while! Is there anything to eat now?" Sarat asked Sita.

"No Sarat. You'll wait till eight o'clock, like everyone else," said Sita.

Sarat's stomach growled, and Sita said, "You will wait! Go practice your Hindi!"

"I've been practicing my Hindi—religiously!" he added.

"You have not taken another lesson in some time. It must mean you are not studying hard enough," said Sita.

"You sound like Prema, hounding Mitch," said Sarat.

"Maybe you want to fast tonight, Sarat?" said Sita, threateningly.

"I meant to say, 'I love you Sita. I love practicing Hindi. I want to practice Hindi right now!' yes that's what I meant to say," said Sarat, changing his attitude.

"Great to hear. If you pass my Hindi test at seven o'clock we'll be able to go to your dad's house for dinner and you'll get another Hindi lesson. Otherwise we may just need to fast and practice Hindi all night long.

"I can hardly wait to see you do well, because I know the food will be so heavenly tonight, if you do!" said Sita.

Mitch looked at her with a stunned look on his face.

"Or maybe you're ready to test now?" said Sita, threateningly.

"No. Not right now. I'll be ready by seven. Yeah...by seven I should be good. Yeah...by seven," repeated Sarat.

"Seven it is then...

"Oh, and Sarat?" said Sita.

"Yes Sita?" he asked.

"You're going to love this sabji korma!" said Sita.

Sarat knew Sita well enough to know she was serious about her implicit threats. He immediately went into the front room, said a prayer to Swarasvati[1], and began immersing himself in all that Sita had taught him.

Sita, meanwhile cooked up the most aromatic food ever to be put into existence. At least that's what Sarat thought, sitting there hungry and engaged in his studies.

Sita's cooking was heavenly, and Sarat had to admit to himself, somewhere in his thoughts, that he was attached to her culinary artistic abilities.

"It's seven o'clock!" said Sita, walking into the front room.

"I know, I'm almost ready," said Sarat.

"How much longer? You've had over a month since the last lesson. You've had enough time," she said, opening up her backpack and pulling out her notebook.

"Here's the test. Take it now, Sarat. Next time you'll think twice about not taking your lessons seriously," she said, handing him the test.

"You have ten minutes," she said.

"Only ten? Why only ten?" asked Sarat.

"It's about to be nine minutes," said Sita in response.

Sarat stopped arguing, and begun.

"Ten minutes for only ten questions, is why!" said Sita, after he started to work.

Sarat didn't pay her any attention. He was hoping he was getting the answers correct.

At eight minutes forty-six seconds he declared, "Finished!"

Sita said nothing. She took his exam and looked over each answer carefully.

"आप को तैयार हैं ?"पूछा|

"हाँ मुझे तैयार हूँ ,सीताजी "|सूरत कहा|

Had he gotten any wrong, he wouldn't be eating most likely. He was inside himself very happy he'd gotten them correct.

As they pulled into Sarat's dad's place, Sita handed the dish she had prepared to Sarat to bring up the flight of stairs. She then started let him lead.

Once upstairs, Sarat knocked on the door. Mitch answered saying, "Hey brother. Glad to see you. Come on in both of you."

Sita said, "Namaste Mitch," politely, and entered in to find the girls. Mitch, after she passed, slipped out onto the outside deck, pulling Sarat aside for a private meeting.

"Sarat, listen, they're not in the best of moods. They've been ganging up on me all day. I said some things to Prema, which weren't even all that hurtful, and she went crazy on me. She's got it in her mind to punish me by having me studying for hours after we eat. They haven't let me eat anything all day hardly. Also, even Ahita is taking sides against me favoring instead to be on Prema's side. Siya is doing the same. Oh, and get this…Michelle too! Even she is taking sides against me and agreeing with Prema.

"Anyway, I'm telling you all this so you know what's up!" said Mitch.

"You think that's bad! Listen to this…

"I almost had to fast all day. Had I not gotten a 100% on a ten question Hindi exam she handed me, I wouldn't even be here nor would I be eating. Instead I'd be humbly studying Hindi all night long, until I passed out from hunger exhaustion!" expressed Sarat.

"Well, dang, that is bad. So basically what you're saying is Sita's in a mood also. This means we're having dinner with five mean girls. You want to just run up to the restaurant, real quick, and grab a bite? We could sneak out now, and probably be back in time before we're missed," said Mitch.

"I would, but I hate to think what would happen if we did get caught. Also, they did go to such a great trouble to cook, we might as well enjoy it. Sita made sabji korma, and it's awesome," shared Sarat.

"Alright. One last thing though… Can I stay with you and Sita tonight? The girls are all staying over and I need a break from them. Plus Prema has it in her head that I'm not studying hard enough, and so I don't want to be up solving math problems all night long. Please say yes!" said Mitch.

"Actually, Sita said we're staying the night over here too! Maybe we can get out of studying. I'll suggest we watch a Hindi movie or something. The girls love playing board games. There's plenty here. Maybe they'll just let you and me hang out by ourselves, while they do girl things. I'm sure we'll come up with something," said Sarat.

"Okay, I'm just glad that you're staying here. I need you here bro!" said Mitch, putting his arm around his brother's neck, leading him into the warm apartment.

"Come let's go to my room," suggested Mitch.

"Okay, but I want to find out how much longer before dinner's ready. I'll be right there," Sarat said to him.

Mitch didn't even want to see the girls. He wanted his sanity. So he went straight to his room. Sarat on the other hand made his way to the kitchen.

"Namaste Prema. Namaste Siya. Namaste Ahita. Namaste Sita," said Sarat to all of them, holding his hands together in front of his chest.

Looking at him they all said, "Namaste Sarat."

"Wow! Everything smells delicious. How much longer till we eat?" asked Sarat; speaking generally to all of them.

"Sarat it will not be much longer. Why don't you go find Mitch and bring him in here," said Prema.

"Sure. I'll be right back," said Sarat.

While Sarat went back to his old bedroom to fetch Mitch, Ahita said to the girls, "Mitch told me yesterday he is ready for namakarana samskara. I am so happy he is taking a Hindu name finally. "पापा ', मिच अपने नामकरना संस्कार होने के बाद वह शादी में अपने हाथ के लिए मुझसे पूछ सकते हैं ने कहा,' लेकिन मिच मैं शायद. आप लड़कियों को इसके बारे में मिच लिए बात कर सकते हैं में से एक बता सकते हैं कि शादी करने के लिए किसी भी सोचा नहीं दिया है? करो इस मामले के बारे में मिशेल बता नहीं. वह कम सूक्ष्म हो सकता है. मैं उसे यह मेरा विचार है नहीं करना चाहती. वह अपने दम पर प्रस्ताव पेश करने चाहिए. मान गया?" Ahita प्रेमा, सीता, और सिय को कहा.

"मिच निश्चित रूप से अधिक पति सामग्री बनता जा रहा है. वह अभी भी एक नौकरी की जरूरत है. शायद सीता उसे वह काम करता है, जहां एक नौकरी मिलने के बारे में सूरत के लिए बात कर सकते हैं. आप क्या सीता लगता है?" प्रेमा पूछा.

"मैं निश्चित रूप से इसके बारे में सूरत से बात करेंगे. वह पूछता है तुम से पहले मैं निश्चित रूप से मैं भी आज रात के लिए कहेंगे. वह वहाँ कुछ शक्ति है तो Ahita. सूरत एक प्रबंधक है, मिच एक नौकरी की जरूरत है," सीता के जवाब दिए.

"What are you saying?" asked Michelle.

"I was only saying how happy I am for Mitch," said Ahita.

Michelle didn't know what the purpose of them speaking in Hindi was, but she suspected there was something discussed, which they didn't want her knowing about. She didn't care, however, and so just dismissed it.

"I would like to adopt a Hindu name too. Michelle is so western, and all of my friends now have Hindu names, so I should also. I am Hindu now, after all," said Michelle.

"That is a wonderful thought," said Sita.

"I agree with Sita. Michelle, you should also have your namakarana samskara soon," said Prema.

"Well, I don't even know how to go about it," she confessed.

"Not to worry. We will help explain to the priest," and he will perform it for you. When are you thinking?" asked Siya.

"Anytime is great!" Michelle said.

"How would tomorrow night be?" suggested Siya.

"I'm fine with that," Michelle said.

"I'll talk to the priest in the morning after the program, and let you know what he says," said Siya.

"Awesome!" commented Michelle.

"Hey! What's holding those boy? The food is ready now, and they are lollygagging. Maybe we have starved them full and they no longer wish to eat. Michelle, can you check on your brothers?" asked Siya.

"I'll be right back," said Michelle, walking that way.

Mitch and Sarat were hanging out in Mitch's room. Mitch suggested they wait, until the food was ready; else, they might have to endure more criticism.

"Mitch! Sarat! Are you two ready to eat? The food is prepared," said Michelle, standing in front of their closed door.

Mitch opened the door and said, "We'll be right there!" He then shut the door softly.

"Come on brother, It's finally ready. I'm starving. Let's go eat," said Mitch.

"I'm with you on that," said Sarat.

When boys fall in love, they are just as much hypnotized as when girls do. Their minds become clouded and they only think of the girl, and little else. It is almost like you're in a dream world. Thinking emotionally, and feeling the reciprocation of those feeling by the person you love.

After being with someone for a while life's repetitions start to subtly happen, without you taking notice. At some point you may awaken and find that you're life has become a habit. Maybe you don't know why you do the things you do—yet you do!

"Wash your hands Mitch," said Ahita.

"You too Sarat," said Prema.

Both boys didn't argue. They just did as they were told. They were famished, Hypnotized to the food they were about to eat. The food they had, had to wait all day long to eat. Their energy was low.

A lot of times in cults, one of the strategies employed is withholding food, or feeding new recruits a carb laden diet. This is done to lower their critical thinking faculty, to help them accept new ideas more susceptibly. At this point Sarat and Mitch would have done just about anything the girls asked them to do without argument or hesitation.

Sarat and Mitch took a seat. They were finally about to eat. All of the girls served the two boys. The boys couldn't get enough food. They were shoveling it down nearly as fast as the girls could serve it.

"Sarat, do not eat so fast. There is plenty of food, and plenty of time to partake of what we've cooked for you," said Sita.

"Mitch, the same goes for you. You are eating too fast. Slow down, please," said Ahita.

It had taken a while but Ahita had trained Mitch to the point where he was listening to her more and more. Mitch valued her advice. He was in love, and the more in love he became, the more he listened to her requests with favor.

Prema was feeling very happy for Sita and Ahita. They had all become close friends, and Prema was proud that the boys had culturally changed to become more Hindu in their thinking. It was a combined effort of all the girls that had influenced this.

After the boys had eaten for some time, the girls served themselves a plate, and took a seat around the kitchen table. Everyone was quietly reflecting on Krishna, and prayerfully eating their food.

After eating Mitch suggested they play a board game together. Prema had other idea, as did Sita.

"Sarat, Prema is going to help Mitch with his schooling. I told you before we left, I had another Hindi lesson for you tonight. Then we need to get a good night's sleep, because we're all going to the temple tomorrow morning together," Sita told him.

"Can we not play a board game first, and then study, and then sleep Sita? What do you think Mitch?" said Sarat looking in his direction.

"I think we would have time for that," he answered.

"No board games!" reiterated Prema. "Now let's go buster," said Prema, demandingly.

"Come on Sarat. I'll teach you in the front room, while Prema teaches Mitch at the kitchen table," Sita said.

Michelle and Siya just smiled at each other. Michelle was thinking how wrapped around their fingers her brothers were. This was never the case growing up with them. They were completely changed from then.

Michelle, Ahita, and Siya cleaned up while Sita and Prema gave lessons.

"Sarat, today's lesson is on verbs. You've learned that they conjugate by adding a stem to the root. You've learned that the infinitive form is the root plus ना you've also learned the simple present and past tenses. Now we'll learn some more, which will free up your ability to communicate much more effectively. You are ready, right?" Sita asked.

"Yes. I'm ready," said Sarat, mentally getting himself prepared to learn another Hindi lesson.

Lesson 7

Sarat, Hindi has several common verb tenses. But, before I teach you about the most common verb tenses, I want to talk to you about the infinitive verb, on last time. The infinitive verb is the verb with the stem ना added to the verb root—for example, the verb बोलना which means 'to speak' contains the root बोल plus the stem ना added. In order to conjugate verbs and use them appropriately, you must first drop the stem, leaving behind only the root, then append a new stem according to Hindi's conjugation rules. The new stem added will correspond with the gender, and number, as it relates to the subject doing the 'acting'.

If we go back to the example of बोलना we can drop the infinitive ending ना, leaving only the root, i.e. बोल, and change it to whatever is required. If, for example, we want to speak an action in the masculine, present simple tense, with the subject being मैं; thus, if we want to say in Hindi, 'I speak' we simply take the root बोल and add the new stem ता, making it बोलता. Because our rules tell us we need the auxiliary (secondary helping verb), we must make it: मैं बोलता हूँ। (I speak.).

These rules are for conjugating intransitive verbs. These are verbs that do not take a direct object. Transitive verbs, on the other hand, do take a direct object. Intransitive verbs must take the post position ने whenever conjugating them; however, only when in the case of the tenses: (a) past simple, (b) present perfect, and (c) past perfect.

The post position will be added immediately after the subject, while the subject will take the oblique form (like all they do with all post-positions added). If, the transitive verb has a direct object the verb must agree with the object in both number and gender. If there isn't a direct object stated in the sentence, then the verb will default to the masculine singular form. It is also important to note how the auxiliary verbs will also have to agree with the object, and not the subject in transitive conjugations.

Sarat, the following tables will shows our example बोलना being represented as a regular verb, and conjugated into the various common Hindi verb tenses. Most Hindi verbs are 'regular' verbs. This is important to understand, because most of the verbs you'll come across in Hindi will take on the following conjugation forms. This makes it simple to know how to conjugate verbs easy in Hindi, given most of them are regular verbs. All you must do is simply learn and remember the predictable patterns to know how to speak actively in Hindi.

On the other hand, there are five primary irregular verbs which should be learnt immediately. These are common verbs that you will use in everyday Hindi conversations. So you must learn them now Sarat. These five verbs are: (a) जाना (to go), (b) करना (to do), (c) लेना (to take), (d) देना (to give), and (e) पीना (to drink). To help you learn these conjugations, and other irregular verb conjugations, I have made for you a table below the regular verb table. I have used, as an example for you, the irregular verb जाना as it is the most common irregular verb you will need to know. It is also an intransitive verb. Do not take tension

Sarat, because the conjugations for irregular verbs, are only slightly different than they are for regular verb conjugations.

So here are some fairly common verbs I have provided for you to practice memorizing and conjugating. Also, below are the table for regular and irregular verbs, which contain the most common conjugations. After you master these conjugations Sarat, you're Hindi will be much more eloquent and conversational and you'll be able to communicate in a greater capacity, after you master these verb conjugations. You'll actually be fluent in Hindi ji.

Common Infinitive Verb List

A
to ache तरसना
to achieve प्राप्त करना
to act अभिनय करना
to admire प्रशंसा करना
to advance तरक्की करना
to anger गुस्सा होना
to apologize क्षमा मांगना
to apply प्रयोग करना
to argue बहस करना
to arrive आना
to articulate साफ़ बोलना
to ask पूछना
to aspire आकांक्षा करना
to avoid दूर रहना

B
to bake सेकना
to bathe स्नान करना
to be होना
to become हो जाना
to bend मोड़ना
to bite काटना
to beg विनती करना
to boast गौरव करना
to borrow उधार लेना
to break तोड़ना
to breathe जीना
to bring लाना
to build निर्माण करना
to buy खरिदना
C
to call बुलाना
to calm शांत करना
to camp पड़ाव डालना
to care चिन्ता करना
to catch पकड़ना
to challenge चुनौती देना
to chill ठण्डा करना
to clap ताली बजाना
to cook पकाना
to collect इकट्ठा करना
to comb कंघी करना
to combine घोलना

to cough	खासना
to cry	रुलाना

D

to dance	नाचना
to deliver	सौंपना
to deny	इन्कार करना
to destroy	नष्ट करना
to devote	समर्पित करना
to dive	गोता लगाना
to do	करना
to doubt	संदेह करना
to dream	कल्पना करना
to dress	सजाना
to drink	पीना
to drive	चलाना
to drop	छोड देना
to dust	झाड़ना

E

to eat	खाना
to eavesdrop	गुप्त वार्ता को सुनना
to embarrass	शर्मिंदा करना
to empty	खाली होना
to energize	क्रियाशील करना
to enter	घुसना
to equal	बराबर होना
to erase	मिटाना
to escape	भाग जाना
to excite	उत्तेजीत होना

to exercise व्यायाम करवाना	
to explain बताना	
to exit बाहर चला जाना	
to extend बढ़ाना	
F	
to face सामना करना	
to fail चूकना	
to faint मुर्झाना	
to fear डरना	
to fight संघर्ष करना	
to film फिल्म बनाना	
to find खोजना	
to fix ठीक करना	
to follow अनुकरण करना	
to forget भूलना	
to forgive क्षमा करना	
to frame विकसीत करना	
to fry तलना	
G	
to gallop सरपट दौड़ाना	
to garden बाग़बानी करना	
to gasp हांफना	
to gaze घूरना	
to get up or rise उठना	
to give देना	
to glisten चमकना	
to gloat बड़ी चाह से देखना	
to go जाना	

to grab	पकड़ना
to grade	अंकित करना
to grind	रगड़ना
to grow	उगाना
to guess	अन्दाज करना

H

to hand	पकड़ा देना
to happen	घटना
to haunt	याद आना
to have	पास होना
to hear	सुनना
to help	सहायता करना
to hesitate	हिचकना
to hire	किराये पर लेना
to hold	पकड़ना
to hop	फुदकना
to hope	आसा करना
to hug	सीने से लगाना
to hurry	जल्दी कराना
to hypnotize	सम्मोहित करना

I

to idolize	पूजना
to ignore	ध्यान न देना
to imagine	सोचना
to immigrate	दूसरे देश में जा बसना
to improve	सुधरना
to include	समावेश करना
to increase	बड़ा करना

to influence	प्रभावित करना
to inspire	उत्पन्न होना
to introduce	परिचय कराना
to invent	अविष्कार करना
to itch	खुजलाना
to interrupt	टोकना
to irritate	चिढ़ाना

J

to jab	कोंचना
to jail	कारावास होना
to jam	अटकना
to jeopardize	जोखिम में डालना
to jingle	खनखनाना
to join	जोड़ना
to joke	मज़ाक करना
to journey	सफर करना
to judge	निर्णय करना
to juggle	बाजीगरी करना
to jump	कूदना
to justify	सत्य ठहराना
to juxtapose	निकट रखना

K

to keel	गिरना
to keep	रखना
to kick	लतियाना
to kid	मजाक करना
to kidnap	अपहरन करना
to kill	समाप्त करना

to kindle	सुलगाना
to kiss	चूमना
to knead	गूँधना
to kneel	घुटने टेकना
to knit	सिकोड़ना
to knock	खटखटाना
to knot	गांठ बांधना
to know	जानना

L

to label	वर्गीकरण करना
to labor	कड़ी मेहनत करना
to land	पहँुचना
to laugh	हसना
to learn	सीखना
to lie	झूठ बोलना
to like	पसन्द करना
to list	इच्छा करना
to listen	सुनना
to live	रहना
to loosen	ढीला करना
to lose	हारना
to love	प्यार करना

M

to mail	डाक करना
to make	बनाना
to manage	संभालना
to map	नक्षा बनाना
to marinate	मसाले के मिश्रण रखना

to mask	छिपाना
to mean	मतलब होना
to meet	मिलना
to measure	मापना
to mellow	सुहावना
to melt	पिघलना
to memorize	याद करना
to modify	परिवर्तन करना
to move	सरकाना

N

to nab	पकड़ लेना
to nail	जकड़ना
to name	नाम रखना
to navigate	जल यात्रा करना
to nap	झपकी लेना
to narrate	सुनाना
to need	चाहना
to neglect	उपेक्षा करना
to nest	घोंसला बनाना
to nod	सिर हिलाना
to notice	ध्यान देना
to nourish	पोसना
to number	गिनना
to nurture	शिक्षा देना

O

to obey	आज्ञा
to observe	निशान करना
to offer	पेश करना

to offend	बुरा लगना
to open	खोलना
to orate	व्यक्त करना
to orchestrate	योजना बनाना
to order	आज्ञा देना
to organize	संघटन करना
to ostracize	निष्कासित करना
to overflow	ऊपर से बहना
to owe	ऋणी होना
to own	अपनाना

P

to paint	सजाना
to parade	जुलूस निकालना
to peel	छीलना
to persuade	विश्वास दिलाना
to photograph	फ़ोटो खींचना
to plant	रोपना
to play	खेलना
to ponder	विचार करना
to practice	अभ्यास करना
to pray	प्रार्थना
to press	दबाना
to promise	प्रतिज्ञा करना
to pretend	मान लेना
to punch	छेदना

Q

to qualify	योग्य ठहराना
to quarrel	झगड़ा करना

to question	सवाल करना
to quiet	शान्त करना
to quit	छोड़ना
to quiz	प्रश्न पूछना
to quiver	काँपना
to quote	उतारना

R

to race	दौड़ लगाना
to rain	वर्षा होना
to ramble	फिरना
to react	विरूद्ध प्रतिक्रिया करना
to rebel	विद्रोह करना
to read	पढ़ना
to relax	आराम करना
to review	निरीक्षण करना
to retire	चला जाना
to rinse	धोना
to rise	उठना
to rule	शासित होना
to run	दौड़ना

S

to sail	जलयात्रा करना
to say	कहना
to sculpt	मूर्ति बनाना
to sell	बेचना
to sing	गाना
to sleep	सोना
to snore	खर्राटा

to surround	घेरना
to speak	बोलना
to spell	सूचित करना
to spill	छलकाना
to spy	अचानक देखना
to stop	रुकना
to swerve	विचलना

T

to take	लेना
to talk	कहना
to tap	हल्का धक्का देना
to taste	चखना
to teach	पढ़ाना
to thank	धन्यवाद करना
to think	सोचना
to tie	बँधना
to toss	उछालना
to touch	छूना
to travel	यात्रा करना
to treat	बर्ताव करना
to trick	छलकपट करना
to try	कोशिश करना

U

to unbuckle	खोलना
to uncover	प्रकाश करना
to undermine	कमज़ोर कर देना
to underlie	आधार होना
to understand	समझना

to unearth	पता लगाना
to unite	एक होना
to unlock	ताला खोल
to unpack	निकालना
to uproot	जड़ से उखाड़ना
to upset	घबरा देना
to untie	खोलना
to use	प्रयोग करना

V

to vacation	छुट्टी बिताना
to vacuum	निर्वात पम्प से साफ़ करना
to vanish	ग़ायब होना
to venture	साहस करना
to verify	जाँचना
to vex	खीजना
to vilify	बदनाम करना
to visit	घूमना
to visualize	देखना
to voice	विचार व्यक्त करना
to volunteer	अपने आप भर्ती होना
to vote	घोषित करना

W

to walk	चलना
to wait	प्रतीक्षा करना
to wander	भटकना
to want	चाहना
to wash	बह जाना
to waste	बर्बाद करना

to wear	पहनना
to welcome	स्वागत करना
to whisper	सफुसाना
to whistle	सीटी बजाना
to wink	आंख मारना
to wonder	जानने को उत्सुक होना
to work	काम करना
to write	लिखना

Y

to yank	झटके से खींचना
to yawn	जम्हाई लेना
to yearn	तरसना
to yell	चिल्लाना
to yelp	चिल्लाना
to yield	समर्पण करना
to yodel	आलापना
to yoke	नाथना

Z

to zero	निशाना लगाना
to zigzag	सर्पिल गति से चलना
to zip	चेन लगाना
to zoom	अचानक बढ़ना

Regular Verb Tenses

	Present Simple (I speak)	Present Continuous (I am speaking)	Present Perfect (I have spoken)
मैं	बोलता हूँ बोलती हूँ	बोल रहा हूँ बोल रही हूँ	बोला हूँ बोली हूँ
तू	बोलता है बोलती है	बोल रहा है बोल रही है	बोला है बोली है
तुम	बोलते हो बोलती हो	बोल रहे हो बोल रही हो	बोले हो बोलीं हो
आप	बोलते हैं बोलती हैं	बोल रहे हैं बोल रही हैं	बोले हैं बोलीं हैं
वो यह	बोलता है बोलती है	बोल रहा है बोल रही है	बोला है बोली है
हम	बोलते हैं बोलती हैं	बोल रहे हैं बोल रही हैं	बोले हैं बोलीं हैं
वे ये	बोलते हैं बोलती हैं	बोल रहे हैं बोल रही हैं	बोले हैं बोलीं हैं

	Past Simple (I spoke)	Past Continuous (I was speaking)	Past Perfect (I had spoken)
मैं	बोला बोली	बोल रहा था बोल रही थी	बोला था बोली थी
तू	बोला	बोल रहा था	बोला था

THE SADHAK • 189

	बोली	बोल रही थी	बोली थी
तुम	बोले बोलीं	बोल रहे थे बोल रही तीन	बोले थे बोलीं तीन
आप	बोले बोलीं	बोल रहे थे बोल रही तीन	बोले थे बोलीं तीन
वो यह	बोला बोली	बोल रहा था बोल रही थी	बोला था बोली थी
हम	बोले बोलीं	बोल रहे थे बोल रही तीन	बोले थे बोलीं तीन
वे ये	बोले बोलीं	बोल रहे थे बोल रही तीन	बोले थे बोलीं तीन

	Past Imperfect (I used to speak)	Future Simple (I will speak)	Future Continuous (I will be speaking)
मैं	बोलता था बोलती थी	बोलूँगा बोलूँगी	बोल रहा हूँगा बोल रही हूँगी
तू	बोलता था बोलती थी	बोलेगा बोलेगी	बोल रहा होगा बोल रही होगी
तुम	बोलते थे बोलती तीन	बोलॉगे बोलॉगी	बोल रहे होगे बोल रही होगी
आप	बोलते थे बोलती तीन	बोलेंगे बोलेंगी	बोल रहे होंगे बोल रही होंगी
वो यह	बोलता था बोलती थी	बोलेगा बोलेगी	बोल रहा होगा बोल रही होगी
हम	बोलते थे बोलती तीन	बोलेंगे बोलेंगी	बोल रहे होंगे बोल रही होंगी
वे ये	बोलते थे बोलती तीन	बोलेंगे बोलेंगी	बोल रहे होंगे बोल रही होंगी

Irregular Verb Tenses

	Present Simple (I go)	Present Continuous (I am going)	Present Perfect (I have gone)
मैं	जाता हूँ जाती हूँ	जेया रहा हूँ जेया रही हूँ	गया हूँ गई हूँ
तू	जाता है जाती है	जेया रहा है जेया रही है	गया है गई है
तुम	जाते हो जाती हो	जेया रहे हो जेया रही हो	गए हो गई हो
आप	जाते हैं जाती हैं	जेया रहे हैं जेया रही हैं	गए हैं गई हैं
वो यह	जाता है जाती है	जेया रहा है जेया रही है	गया है गई है
हम	जाते हैं जाती हैं	जेया रहे हैं जेया रही हैं	गए हैं गई हैं
वे ये	जाते हैं जाती हैं	जेया रहे हैं जेया रही हैं	गए हैं गई हैं

	Past Simple (I went)	Past Continuous (I was going)	Past Perfect (I had gone)
मैं	गया गई	जेया रहा था जेया रही थी	गया था गई थी

तू	गया गई	जेया रहा था जेया रही थी	गया था गई थी
तुम	गए गईं	जेया रहे थे जेया रही तीन	गए थे गईं तीन
आप	गए गईं	जेया रहे थे जेया रही तीन	गए थे गईं तीन
वो यह	गया गई	जेया रहा था जेया रही थी	गया था गई थी
हम	गए गईं	जेया रहे थे जेया रही तीन	गए थे गईं तीन
वे ये	गए गईं	जेया रहे थे जेया रही तीन	गए थे गईं तीन

	Past Imperfect (I used to go)	Future Simple (I will go)	Future Continuous (I will be going)
मैं	जाता था जाती थी	जाऊँगा जाऊंगी	जेया रहा हूँगा जेया रही हूँगी
तू	जाता था जाती थी	जाएगा जाएगी	जेया रहा होगा जेया रही होगी
तुम	जाते थे जाती तीन	जाओगे जाओगी	जेया रहे होगे जेया रही होगी
आप	जाते थे जाती तीन	जाएँगे जाएँगी	जेया रहे होंगे जेया रही होंगी
वो यह	जाता था जाती थी	जाएगा जाएगी	जेया रहा होगा जेया रही होगी
हम	जाते थे जाती तीन	जाएँगे जाएँगी	जेया रहे होंगे जेया रही होंगी
वे	जाते थे	जाएँगे	जेया रहे होंगे

ये	जाती तीन	जाएँगी	जेया रही होंगी

Hindi Verb Types

Now, that you've learnt the various primary tenses in Hindi; namely, that verbs can be regular or irregular, transitive or intransitive, and how all of these factors affect how a verb is conjugated when used in an active sentence. Now, I want to walk you through the various Hindi verb types to help you master conversational Hindi grammar.

So we know that Hindi verbs can be intransitive and transitive; that is, an intransitive verb has no direct object, meaning there is not person or thing inside a sentence which is the recipient of the action verb. For example, we could say, "मैं अस्तित्वा हूँ," denoting, "I exist." You cannot exist a person or thing, thus this verb is intransitive. A transitive verb on the other hand has one or more direct objects. This means the person or thing in the sentence receives the action of the verb. For example: 'वह रॉक चले गए', i.e. 'The rock moved,' is a perfect example of a transitive verb, because something has to be moved, and in this case it is a rock. You can move a person, move a rock, or move just about anything, really, and so Sarat, for this reason this verb is transitive.

Sarat, it is important you understand the difference between transitive and intransitive verbs. One of the easiest ways to practice this is to take the verbs in the dictionary ordered list I presented you with, and go through and discover which are transitive and which are intransitive.

There are also another type of verb called compound verbs. These are multi-part verbs, which consist of a primary very and a 'helping verb' or auxiliary verb. Both verbs work together as a single verb, which is usually used to alter the meaning subtly from its primary verb intention. So the auxiliary verb in a compound conjugation creates a specificity to the primary verb, describing the quality of how that primary verb performs. This adds depth and higher quality to basic Hindi sentences.

I'll demonstrate an example to help you Sarat: मैं बैठ गया. This means: I sat down. Well we know that the infinitive verb बैठना means 'to sit'. But, when we use the compound verb it assumes the root: बैठ along with the auxiliary verb गया (to go), to make it mean: 'sat down'. Sarat, there are many Hindi verbs that are compound. If you pay attention you also notice in this example that only the auxiliary verb is inflected. The root stays as is.

Besides compound verbs there are also conjunct verbs. These are when we take an adjective or noun, and connect it to a verb, to give a nominal conjunct, or adjectival conjunct. When verbs are conjunct, they function as a simply verb. If we take for instance the adjective 'clean' which is साफ़, can be added to verb करता है and made into a sentence like: वह साफ़ करता है. This sentence translated means: He cleans. Many Hindi verb constructions are conjunct verbs. It is easy to identify these verbs because usually the primary verb is करता and the conjunct is a noun or adjective just before it.

Another type of Hindi verb are imperatives. These are verbs used to give a command. We must use discretion when using these verbs because they can be misinterpreted to mean you are being disrespectful. You must for this reason know the person you're talking to when giving this type of command. Your tonality will also be important in your delivery. If you want someone to speak in English, you can say: अंग्रेजी बोलो which means English speak! This is a तुम construction. If you want to make the command less intense and as if you're saying 'please' you can simply add the आप form, i.e. बोलिए. You don't have to include the subject in these constructions, as it's implied already, though you could if you wanted to. It is common to leave the subject out of the imperative construction, that is.

Another type of verb are causal verbs. These verbs represent actions that are indirectly caused by the subject of the sentence. In other words, the subject makes, causes, or enables another person or thing to so do something. These constructions are influencing type. They are also classified as transitive verbs, because something or someone has to cause something to happen. For example: मैंने उससे समझवाया. This verdict takes the intransitive verb: समझाना (to explain), and adds the वा to the root, to make it causal. Thus we end up with मैंने उससे समझवाया| meaning, 'I had him explain'. The subject 'I' is causing someone, i.e. 'him' to do something, which in this case is 'explain' something. Notice also that the subject takes on the post position ने and for this reason goes into the oblique case, as any subject taking on a post position would require.

Sarat, as you master these types of verbs you'll also prepare yourself to learn many other types. You'll also learn as you go, many other types of conjugations. It is a process to master a full range of conjugation and types of verbs.

Notes

[1] Swarasvati is the Hindu Goddess of Learning and Education.

CHAPTER 8

Decisions Decisions

Some time had passed. Sarat had really gotten serious with his Hindi lessons. He was taking every opportunity to talk to his friends in Hindi; that is, the ones who spoke Hindi. Even Prema had commented to Sita about how well-spoken Sarat was when he spoke to her in Hindi.

Mitch had graduated with honors. He was now temporarily working under his brother at the warehouse. Ahita was proud of him, as were his sister Michelle, Prema and Siya. They all seemed to look at Mitch as a helpless person that needed looking after.

Mitch and Michelle had adopted Hindu names. Mitch was named Acyuta, after the 'infallible aspects' of Lord Krishna. Michelle was named Adisvari, which means 'original goddess'.

John, Sarat's father, remarried and was living on the road full time with his new wife. He was happy, and she also. Sometimes it is enough to be in the company of someone you love, and that satisfy your heart's desires.

Sita was committed fully to the household. She kept her and Sarat's apartment clean, cooked their food, and as she did these things she joyously and worshipfully sang and hummed bhajans. She was a dutiful person, and it was clear by her actions alone, she loved Sarat as her own husband. These days, she was speaking Hindi to him, and he was talking to her back in Hindi.

Everyday stayed unnoticeably the same as each day before. This is the life of a sadhak. A sadhak by the way is a spiritual aspirant. Regulation is important for spiritual practice. It keeps a devotee grounded, learning, and leaning on God, and achieving spiritual insights without always wanting to want other things. The highest ideal is God, and for the sadhak it is the only yearning. Whatever enters into one's life, is always secondary to God, and always given secondary importance. Moreover, every secondary importance is honored as God—so everything is God.

Sarat worked hard at his job. He was always, as Big Jake, honoring his work as an opportunity to worship Lord Krishna. When you frame working in this type of context it isn't work at all; rather, always spiritual practice.

After work the young couple spent their time at the mandir, doing their shared spiritual practices, and, from time to time, visiting with other devotees, including, and especially, Acyuta and Adisvari, Prema, Siya, and Ahita.

"What do you mean he wants to get married," asked Sarat, looking questioningly upset at Prema.

"Listen Sarat. Your brother and Ahita are in love, and they want to get married.

"I'm telling you this, because you are the eldest brother, and so it more right that you get married first. You must have proposed to Sita, by now, yes?"

"Listen Prema, I haven't asked Sita yet, because I'm afraid she'd say no," admitted Sarat.

"You silly boy, you make everything so complicated. It is November, a perfect time for a Hindu wedding. You're not to worry about a thing, I will help you. No worries ji," assured Prema, smiling devilishly.

"Now Prema, I don't want you messing around in our affairs. I've been down that road before, and I don't want any more stress or worries," warned Sarat.

"I got you Sarat. Absolutely ji. Everything will be okay, not to worry. I got you!

"Hey, listen Sarat, I have to run, and I'll see you back at the mandir tonight. Take no tension at all. Not to worry. I got this. No worries whatsoever. No worries," Prema kept reiterating as she took off in another direction to some place unknown.

Sarat could hear Prema's words hypnotizing him, as the words muted out the farther away Prema became. In his mind he knew better. He knew Prema always had a good intent, usually, but, he also knew the other side of her nature, which was usually to take over and take dominance over other peoples' affairs. He hoped he wouldn't have to take tension or worry about a thing, because he hoped Prema would just forget, and keep her nose out of it.

Prema Talks to Sita

"I am serious Sita, my parents want to help," ensured Prema.

"I don't know Prema. Are you sure?" asked Sita.

"I'm sure ji, so what says you? Are you in or out?"

"I am almost unsure, but if you're sure, I'll make myself sure," promised Sita.

"It is settled then. I'll tell mummy and daddy and everything will be fine. No worries," said Prema.

"I am so excited. I had no idea he wanted to marry me. Boys are such cowards, aren't they? Anyway, of course I say yes, but he should ask me himself," decreed Sita.

"He will ask you tonight at the mandir. He will. You'll see," Prema insisted.

Sita was smiling as Prema pulled out of the parking lot. Sarat was still at work, working hard on getting ready for the upcoming holiday season—the busiest time of year for the warehouse.

Later that evening, when Sarat arrived home, Sita explained to him how they would be eating at Prema's parent's house tonight after temple.

"What brought this about?" questioned Sarat.

"I don't know, she just extended the invitation, and I accepted for us."

"What do you make of it though?" asked Sarat, trying to get more information.

"I don't make anything of it Sarat. We'll see, when we see."

"Yeah, but she must have said something?" he pressed.

"She did. I told you. Have you not been listening to me? Prema told us her parents have invited us for dinner after temple tonight. I accepted their invitation. It was a kind invitation. Nothing more," reiterated Sita.

In his mind Sarat was confused, trying to make sense of the sudden unexpected invitation by Prema's parents. It had been several weeks since he last spoke to Prema, and now all this, and for what, he wondered. By the minute he was growing more nervous and more nervous.

When the young couple finally reached the temple, Prema was laughing in the parking lot with Ahita, Siya, and Adisvari. As Sita and Sarat approached them, the girls started giggling.

It was somehow infectious giggling, because Sita also started to giggle.

"What's so funny?" questioned Sarat.

The answer didn't come.

After the Bhagavad Gita discourse, Prema abruptly interrupted a conversation Sarat was having with his brother Acyuta. "Excuse me Acyuta, can I borrow your brother Sarat for a moment?" asked Prema standing over the two brothers who were seated in one corner of the mandir.

"Sure, leave me lonely, Prema," joked Acyuta.

"You're not lonely, Ahita is coming now, and you'll never be lonely with the way she looks at you," said Prema, getting back at him.

Acyuta just blushed. It was true: Ahita was making her way in that direction.

"What is it Prema?" asked Sarat, half afraid to leave with her.

"I'll tell you in private. Come with me," she implored.

Sarat stood up, adjusted his dhoti and kurta, and took her side and followed her into the adjoining café.

Upon entering, noticing nobody was inside, Prema took them to a table in one of the back corners.

"Okay, here's the deal. I talked with Sita. You're not supposed to know this, but I'm on your side here, and as I told you before, I would help you.

"Sita wants you to propose to her tonight, in fact now, here at the mandir. Tonight, at dinner, my parents have a gift for you both.

"See I told you I would come through for you! I am so excited for you both. So very excited.

"Anyway, come on, we have to go," Prema demanded.

"Wait! So you're saying, Sita expects me to propose now? I don't even know how to go about this? I haven't even had time to think this through, you know?"

"Come on ji, you have to ask her. You both are in love. You cannot keep a girl waiting indefinitely. You have a job. You live together, even. It is time you manned up and made a decision. Now is the time. What will it be? You don't get a second chance Sarat," Prema chided him.

"I don't know. I just feel like I'm rushing this whole marriage thing. I'm..."

"You're being childish Sarat. Also selfish. What about Sita's feelings? You have asked me to help you. I have upheld my promise..."

"Wait just a minute Prema. I never asked for your help in the first place. You just took it upon yourself to..."

"What are you two talking about?" asked Siya, approaching them.

"Sarat is going to ask Sita to marry him now. Do you want to come watch him ask?" Prema said to Siya.

Sarat was stricken with embarrassment.

"Come on Sarat, I forgive you for hurting my feelings with those hurtful words, but now it's time to prove your love for Sita. Come on," insisted Prema.

"What are you three doing in here?" asked Adisvari, walking up too.

"Your brother is going to propose marriage to Sita right now. Do you want to come watch him become a man?" asked Prema.

"Oh wow. It is about time Sarat. We've all been talking and wondering when you would ask Sita. Surely she is more than ready to say yes. I am so happy for you." Adisvari exclaimed.

"Well..."

"Everything is well. As promised! So come, let's go now," insisted Prema standing up.

Sarat was once again outnumbered. The girls were running the show, it seemed.

As Prema and the other girls led Sarat over to Sita, who was sitting in a corner of the mandir, talking with Ahita and Acyuta, laughing it up over some silly talk, noticing the entourage and her man Sarat coming, Sita quieted as did Acyuta and Ahita.

As typical, Prema took the lead. And, Sarat was for once glad she did. His nerves were shot, and he'd never been more nervous in his entire life.

"Namaste Sita," greeted Prema, taking a seat inside the group. Sarat and the other girls followed and joined the group too.

"Namaste Prema," said Sita smiling.

"Listen Sita, Sarat has something he is dying to ask you. Sarat, ask her," said Prema, putting him on the spot in front of the group.

Sita just sat there starting straight into the eyes of Sarat, with love reflected in her eyes.

"Sita, I have been thinking lately, how we are living together, and still not married. I wanted to ask you a long time ago, but I was too afraid. Now I'm not afraid, so I want to ask you to be my wife. Will you marry me?" asked Sarat, half relieved, half afraid of Sita's response.

Sita let him remain afraid, as she took her time answering him back. Finally, she said, "Yes."

The girls started giggling as they had been outside the mandir earlier. Acyuta pushed his brother's arm and said, "Congratulations brother!" with excitement in his voice.

Sarat was never happier. Sita had agreed to marry him, and it was priceless in terms of value. He loved her immeasurably. She loved him the same way. Sita even began crying, which caused Sarat to cry also. Sarat had always seen her strong, but now it was obvious she was letting her emotions out into the ether, unafraid to be afraid anymore, and perhaps because she was in-love with the boy she loved.

Dinner is Served with a Priceless Gift

At the Hindmarch's house, Prema and her mother served the guests, and everyone was there: Sarat, Sita, Acyuta, Ahita, Siya, and Adisvari. Also present was Mr. Hindmarch.

The suspense about what was to be discussed over dinner was almost killing Sarat. He had no clue what was about to go-down.

"Okay, so first, I'd like to pose a toast—to Sarat and Sita's marriage proposition. I have seen big changes out of both you young people in the last few years. You have proven, albeit I don't agree with young people living together before marriage, but that's another matter for another time, that you two are made for each other.

"I have discussed this with Prema and my wife for quite some time and we've decided to bestow some of our good fortune, onto you.

"Meaning, we are paying for your wedding," Mr. Hindmarch announced.

"I..." said, Sita

"I..." said, Sarat

Both talking simultaneously, interrupting one another.

"You go ahead, Sarat," said Sita.

"I, I mean we, I mean, I guess I don't know what I mean, but I don't know what to say, Mr. Hindmarch. It is hard to accept such a large gift."

"That's because there's nothing to talk about, except where do you want to have the wedding?" Mr. Hindmarch retorted.

"That's actually the problem sir. Sarat and I wanted to get married in India. We've actually talked about moving there permanently. There's no way we could manage this right now, with our financial situation, and there's no way we can expect you to help us with this dilemma. I have faith though that eventually it will happen, and we'll able to have our wedding there," said Sita.

"My dear, I don't think you quite understand. My family is paying for your wedding. I think a proper Hindu wedding in India, would be for the best.

"As I've explained we're taking care of everything wedding related, including everyone's airfare. Everything Sita. Your only concern should be Prema—she likes to take over everything—don't you princess?" said Mr. Hindmarch, tittering.

Everyone started laughing—even Prema.

After dinner and more discussion over the matter, it was decided that the wedding would take place in Nerul, in Navi-Bombay, the last week of November. Mr. Hindmarch owned both commercial and residential real estate there, and he already knew of the perfect wedding hall. The hall was near many Hindu temples, which Sita could decide on for the main ceremony. Mr. Hindmarch also had homes which would accommodate everyone with a place to stay. It was perfect.

CHAPTER 9

भारत - मेरे घर

There was never a more beautiful wedding. Sita cried, Sarat cried, and every eye in the mandir cried it seemed. I wasn't exactly there.

The young couple found themselves in a new apartment—one that the Hindmarch's had owned and gifted them with as a wedding present.

The first night they were permitted to stay in the new apartment was their wedding night. Sarat had carried Sita through the threshold of the apartment for good luck, and the though the night went awkward, the couple being physically intimate with each other for the first time, it was something beautiful and to remember always for both of them.

In the morning Sita awoke at three o'clock, and seeing Sarat still sleeping, awoke him so they could begin their first day together in the new apartment. There was so much to be done.

"Sarat, come, it's time to get-up," urged Sita.

Sarat didn't say anything. He was sort of hypnotized from not getting much sleep, and from being disoriented from his new surroundings. This apartment was nothing like their slum-apartment which they had lived in back in Chicago for all that time.

The morning went rather well. Sita and Sarat bathed, did sadhana, Sita prepared them breakfast, and afterward they went walking about Nerul.

Their apartment they came to realize was in a perfect location. Only two blocks from in front of train station. The main train coming into and out of Nerul would take them straight into the heart of Bombay, that is, right to C.S.T., which from there they could then catch any train to take them anywhere they wished to go in Bombay—even the remote suburbs.

Beyond the train station, passing through onto the other side of the platforms, was a small road, which inclined up a steeply graded hill. Walking up the hill, the couple noticed a beautiful nature park on the left, with paths to explore and no traffic or congestion. It seemed to them the calm in the storm of what at first Nerul seemed to them.

Nerul was busy, though nowhere near a busy at other parts of Bombay. Still the cars passing by, honking horns, many people in the streets, and literally no privacy, seemed surprisingly busier than Chicago, and the not-so-nice neighborhood they lived in before.

Further up the hill, on both sides of the road, were many temples. One of the temples seemed very peaceful to Sita, so they took an interest in exploring its grounds. It was a Goddess temple, one dedicated to Goddess Amritanandamayi, and incarnation of the Goddess Lalita. Sita, found a cool spot to sit, and Sarat sat down near beside her. Then Sita suggested they pray, chanting the thousand names of the *Rahasya Nama Sahasra* (Secret Names 1000), or what is more normally named, *Lalita Sahasranama Stotram*. This is what the young couple prayed every day, and knew by memory. Together they prayed this hymn, and worshipped the Great Goddess Lalitambika.

When they finished they approached the murti, took darshana, and quietly and reflectively walked back down the hill, back to their apartment.

"I'll make us some lunch," Sita said.

"Alright, I'll check to see if the Internet is working, yet," said Sarat.

It was new place, new surroundings, they both were out of their element, and by now, Acyuta, Ahita, Prema, Siya, Adisvari, and Prema's parents were aboard an airplane, if not yet arrived back in Chicago yet. Everyone had stayed in a bungalow owned by the Hindmarch's over in sector 21, but it was now empty, only tended to by servants, and everyone was gone now.

It left a bit of an emptiness inside Sarat, because he was not expected to work in a strange new land, to take care of Sita, and to carry them into the future safely and soundly. It is a lot of responsibility.

Sita on the other hand, she was expected to tend to the home, prepare the meals, activate spiritual disciplines, and eventually be the best mother for their children.

Fortunately, for Sarat, he discovered a secret unknown truth, that was only a week earlier made known to him. The warehouse he had been working in management at was actually one of Mr. Hindmarch's businesses. Mr. Hindmarch also owned a massive warehouse in Bombay, right near the ports. The ports of Bombay are largest in India, and account for a huge margin of the Gross Domestic Product in India. Business literally would stop if these ports ever stopped importing and exporting goods.

Now, Sarat would be being paid in US dollars, at a wage higher than he was making in the US warehouse. Only, his money would carry him and Sita much further, as the exchange rate was 51 Rs. per dollar. Things were much cheaper in India, and his wage was high, even for a US wage. The young couple would be well off, in India it seemed.

CHAPTER 10

The Last Chapter

It wasn't an easy life, by any means. The young couple, accordingly lived in India, raised a family of two girls, and grew old together. I was tired in the end.

Life is ordinary, and yet not. There's always ups and downs, frets and flows, and love and hate situations. It is the nature of creation, preservation, and destruction.

As humans we're limited in what we can observe at any given moment. For this reason, alone, we cannot always occupy our minds with all things necessary to focus on. Just as soon as we have created something beautiful, done our best to preserve it, we've destroyed it; because we have focused on something else.

Had we kept our focus, only on our regulated life, the live which is our religion, we'd have discovered our true happiness—always sustained—as infinitely so as some oblivion, where nothing exists at all.

This young couple, we abided by the dharma given us at birth, and remained in love from day one. In love with God. Nothing mortal is water-tight. Everything has holes in it, even if your eyes lie to you. The only constant, which never diminishes, or loses luster, is love.

When I learnt Hindi, all those years ago, it was for reasons of love. When I endured the cold Chicago Winters, it was for reasons of love. When I entered the gateway of India, to call it my home, it was for reasons of love. Beyond the upsets, the drawbacks, the missed opportunities, and the lost fortunes, there exists only love.

You need only close your eyes, imagining what you will; what life you want, what involvements you wish to experience, and you will, in that very moment, have those happenings happening to you. Happy and sad are but only an illusion. Words are only logical relay-ments of faulty rationalizations. The only exception being the Language of God. When you learn this language no other language will constrain your meanings. Just even thinking the words will cause your emotions to spiral into a state of spiritual awakening—some Hypnosis.

It took me a long time, longer than any other book, to write this book. I couldn't figure out why, until now.

This perplexed me, it drove me insane, it haunted me like a bad thought that won't go away, and finally in the end it became my salvation, my finest hour.

I saw her lying there. It was highly unusual given she had awaken me nearly every day, since I met her, many years ago, and now when she needed me to awaken her, I was unable to—I failed.

My eyes wept. My body grew cold, like hers. And I was, half-dead in that instant, and I knew it.

The funeral was a pyre of burning woods, and the ashes found their way through me into the Ganges of Banaras, and just as I finished my last word, which were: मैं उसके बगल में गंगा में, मैं मर गया.

The pen fell into the cold water, along with his cold lifeless body, and I retrieved his letters, which were saved from the fate of illegibility, from what would have been a watery death. I quickly, ran home, to my apartment and began to write the words he'd written. They were all in Hindi, and the translation, though not perfect, captured the intent.

My eyes wept, learning of his life, but not for sadness sake; rather, because I loved this man I never knew, this man I call—The Sadhak.

THE POSTLOGUE

The Man I Call Sadhak & His Hindi Lessons

I nearly, left this postlogue out of the book. I am not your typical writer, by any means. I don't know always what to write next. This was the case with this book. I started this book in January, 2014, and stopped in March 2014, and only began again today, before I finished. This should tell you by inference alone, that the book was nearly finished, when I stopped it back in March.

The characters, they come alive in my mind. I'm a spiritual writer, and there's overtones to this fact in my writings. I don't take credit for the spiritual aspects, because they just happen. I'm sometimes drawing a line in the sand, I refuse to cross, and find myself crossing it anyway. I can't help this, because I don't always write the words myself.

The characters in this book are to me as real as you the reader; only I know them better, and for this reason they seem more real to me than you. I want you to know them, as I know them, though I know you never will, but I pray I'm wrong, for your sake.

The Hindi lessons in this book are to help you learn Hindi. The lessons are not exhaustive, but will teach you the basics, and thus basic fluency. It's up to you to learn the lessons, then learn more, or not. I have intentionally left some of the book in Hindi, without translation, to encourage the reader to find the meaning out on his own volition. I've done this to encourage you in your Hindi learning. Whenever something is left incomplete, one experiences the Zeirgarnik Effect, which causes you to feel, and forever, incomplete. To the extent you wish to know the characters, dream in Hindi, and in time, assuming you have not already, which if you're reading this book I must assume, you'll learn the Language of God.

I have to be careful in how I communicate these final words, because they can be perceived, to those who know not, as though their condescending. That is not how I intention them to be. If everything you do is for LOVE, you're doing something right, and paradoxically—not so right. It is challenging for me to dispel to you in English, what I mean. I'm bound by the rules of Grammar, but not the Language of God, which are juxtaposed and set against these words, if you're willing and receptive to insightfully realizing them.

I truly hope you have received more than just an education in Hindi, while reading this book. If you have, you'll more likely desire to speak Hindi, more and more, and perhaps wish to speak less English. You see there's some secrets nested in these pages. Some I don't even know.

Some I have discovered. The Sadhak, if you'll let him, will speak to you, in a language other than English.

On a final note: I may create some flashcards for this book, I'm still not sure. If so, you'll find them at:

www.indirectknowledge.com

About The Author

Bryan James Westra is author of over a dozen books. He's a Hindi and Sanskrit scholar, Hypnotist, and NLPer. For more information visit: www.indirectknowledge.com

www.ingramcontent.com/pod-product-compliance
Lightning Source LLC
Chambersburg PA
CBHW032250150426
43195CB00008BA/396